Single Mom Survival Guide: Strategies for Success

Maha J. Sierra

All rights reserved.

Copyright © 2024 Maha J. Sierra

*Single Mom Survival Guide: Strategies for Success :
Empowering Tips for Achieving Triumph as a Solo Mother*

Funny helpful tips:

Join a book club; discussions with others can offer diverse interpretations and insights.

Stay vigilant about tech's impact on mental health; while it connects us, it also poses challenges like screen addiction.

Introduction

This is not just a book; it's a roadmap to empowerment and success for single mothers navigating the challenges of parenthood on their own. Through a series of insightful chapters, this guide offers invaluable advice and encouragement, empowering single moms to embrace their journey with confidence and resilience.

Confidence sets the foundation for success, encouraging single moms to believe in themselves and their abilities. By going beyond what is expected, they can defy stereotypes and exceed their own expectations, showing the world what they're truly capable of.

Teaching the world how to see you is about asserting one's identity and demanding respect. Single moms are encouraged to stand tall and assert their worth, refusing to be defined by societal stigmas or limitations.

Remembering who you are is a powerful reminder to single moms to stay true to themselves amidst the chaos of parenthood. By nurturing their own identity and passions, they can maintain a sense of balance and fulfillment in their lives.

Expanding the mind is essential for personal growth and development. Single moms are encouraged to embrace new experiences, pursue education and self-improvement, and open themselves up to new possibilities.

Money and finances can be a source of stress for single moms, but by taking control of their financial situation and making smart decisions, they can achieve stability and security for themselves and their children.

Being your own best friend means treating yourself with kindness and compassion, especially during challenging times. Single moms are reminded to prioritize self-care and seek support when needed.

Stigmas surrounding single motherhood are addressed head-on, challenging stereotypes and advocating for respect and understanding. By rewriting their own happily ever after, single moms can create a fulfilling and joyful life for themselves and their children.

Finally, keeping your tools sharp is about staying prepared and adaptable in the face of life's challenges. Single moms are encouraged to continuously learn, grow, and evolve, equipping themselves with the skills and resilience needed to overcome any obstacle.

With its empowering message and practical advice, this book is a must-read for any single mother looking to build a bright and fulfilling future for herself and her family.

Contents

Tool #1: Confidence 1
My relationship with Confidence 6
Shining a light in dark places 8
To love yourself completely, you must first know yourself 10
Step One: Recognize It 11
Make a Choice 12
The Ego is your BFF 14
Overview 17
Tool #2: Going Beyond What IsExpected 18
The Busy Badge 21
Shooting Star 23
Are you going beyond? 27
Number One 28
Number Two 32
Number Three 34
Perception is QUEEN 34
Tool #3: Teach The World How To SeeYou 37
Click-Clonk and Support Husbands 38
Show Up 40
Teaching the World 44
1. Slow. Your. Roll. 44
2. Ask Questions…All the Questions 46
3. Dream Out Loud 48
This is for you 49
Tool #4: Remember Who YouAre 51
Journey 53
Like a Virgin 57
Stop Shrinking 58
Look Me in the Eye 60
Walk your Walk 61

Hugs over Handshakes	62
Summary	63
Tool #5: Expand Your Mind	65
Webster	69
Read-Read-Read	70
Meditation	72
Journal	73
The company you keep	75
Deconstructing Limiting Beliefs, Limited Thinking, and Tomatoes	78
Tool #6: Money and Finances	82
Enough	85
Planning	87
The 4 Step Easy-Peasy Approach	87
Working the Plan	91
My Personal Thoughts and Reflections on Financial Planning	93
Triggers	94
Rainy Days	95
Finding Support	95
Let it be Simple	96
Closing	97
Tool #7: Be Your Own Best Friend	98
The Inner Critic	102
Drop the Negativity	105
One is not a lonely number	107
Tool #8:	111
Soccer Moms	111
Societal Stigmas	116
Let people know when they are stigmatizing	119
Empowerment over Shame	120
Get support	121
This too shall pass	122
Tool #9: Rewrite Your Happily Ever After	123
I Love You Forever	125

Dating, Hooking Up, and Hanging Out	128
Frayed Yarn	133
We went to Jared's	138
Tool #10: Keep Your Tools Sharp	143
Obsessions and Illusions	145
Flexibility, Ebbing, and Flowing	146
Humility and Pride	149

Tool #1: Confidence

I sat there cross legged on the side of the fence. It wasn't strange or abnormal. This was always one of my favorite places as a girl. I would take opportunities to visit the farm as often as I could, whether it was with my grandpa to check on the goats and give the cows hay, or with my parents to place a saddle on the horse and take a trip out to the field. I remember the smells of hay, alfalfa particularly. A weedy, sweet scent that seemed to linger softly in the air, mixed with the aroma of farm animals and moldy pond water.

It never fails to amaze me to think about the things we notice when we're young. The shades of things. The corners. The way the light hits the ground. The texture of grass. As I write this, I can't help but question: If I were to find myself sitting on that fence today, would I still notice these things? Not likely. Maybe I would be too caught up in the oceans of my own mind with some stale storyline that I chose to narrate about my job, my kid's teacher, or a family member. I'd be playing out some petty drama that would suck my attention out of the beauty of the moment like a silent vacuum, ruthless and unapologetic.

Nonetheless, in my child's eye, I would wait on the side of that fence for someone to beckon me to help with a chore or to pet one of the animals. But on this particular day, the farm and my spot on the fence shaped a different meaning and memory that I could hold onto like a warm hand for years to come.

I am unsure of the rationale behind his decision to make this the day I needed to learn to jump off the side of a horse while it galloped at full speed, you know, in the event of an emergency. Now this might seem perfectly logical at first read, but let me insert here that I was not even five years old at the time. And we are talking about a full-grown horse, which means my young body is over five feet in the air.

My dad's intentions were pure, and I believe that what he wanted me to learn that day was how to protect myself if I ever got into a bad situation on the back of a horse. It was that simple in his mind. When life presented an opportunity for me to learn a life lesson, he would throw me right into the deep end. Quite literally. I learned how to swim just a year prior to that very day while when on a family vacation. He decided I was old enough to know how to swim and tossed me into the deep end of the motel pool without my floaties. This is one of those memories that becomes etched in the recesses of your mind. I can still see it from an outsider's perspective. It was dark outside, my aunts and uncles sat around the pool with cold cans of beer and their hands, I had been swimming for hours, my white blonde hair hanging wet and matted all around my face, my bright blue bathing suit with white straps hugging my tan little body as I flew through the air to meet the fate waiting below—the deep end of the pool. All I know for certain is that I swam, and I never needed floaties after that night.

So, it should not come as a surprise there we were again in a similar situation. He wanted me to learn something and there was no time for lessons or professionals. We would be hitting it head-on.

Let's not try to reason out the judgements here. We only know that somewhere in his nothing but an adolescent mind, he thought that day was somehow the perfect time for me to learn to jump off of a horse. Yes. Full jump. Off the back of a full-grown horse.

In hindsight, maybe I should be writing this passage about the fact that I was not quite five and I rode horses often in the field next to our trailer with my parents, racing them at full gallop from end to end. Riding that fast didn't scare me, though. What scared me was the prospect of jumping down from this very gigantic animal that made me feel much like a giant myself while on her back.

By this point in my young life, I had already figured out I had an aversion to heights. I avoided looking at the ground when I was riding at full speed because it made me dizzy, and the idea of falling seriously terrified me.

If I would have had the ability to articulate myself with reason, I probably could have stopped this from happening altogether. But I had nothing, no words that could possibly form a counter argument for this. All I had was my child brain, my child hands, and my child fear. We were no match for my dad's ideas and determination.

He was very frustrated that I was scared, and the fact that my Mom also had a twinge of second guessing in her voice didn't help matters. If anything, it fueled his resolve that was the day. "By God, we are going to teach this girl to jump off of a horse. If she is going to ride, she needs to know." And so, it would be.

As I gazed up toward the beast of an animal that I had come to love so dearly, a lump formed in my throat. My horse's name was Nail. She was a rich, dark brown and black color and shimmered when the light hit her coat. I dreamed about her often. I felt a connection to her spirit. It seemed I was always waiting with excitement for the next time I'd be able to ride her, to the point my days revolved around "the next time." But not today. Today was nothing but a sense of dread, probably echoing the sort of dread a prisoner felt, walking into a chamber to see their electric chair waiting. I felt like death were imminent and terror built inside me. Hot tears found my cheeks before they could even get me mounted on her back.

The first few jumps were more like me hanging onto Nail's mane and trying to shimmy down the side of her massive body. I believe she sensed what was going on and would slow down and walk a little softer, knowing I was about to slide down her side. I landed on my feet, feeling clever and glad to not have suffered any broken bones, a smile resurfaced on my face. My dad, however, did not share the same enthusiasm with our performance.

Clearly, I was missing the point entirely. I needed to learn how to jump off with the horse in a full gallop, you know, in the face of imminent danger. Again, my child reasoning failed to question the obvious—why would a horse run toward danger? All that mattered was I was failing the lesson. And so, we continued for what seemed like hours.

Bit by bit, I would urge Nail to go faster and I would fall like a dummy off her side, hitting the ground so hard a few times it knocked the air out of my lungs. That was the only time I thought I was dying. I didn't know what it felt like to not have oxygen flowing seamlessly through my body. As scary as it was, it wasn't death, and the act of dying was the only thing that was going to stop this charade.

Back on the horse I went, circling the meadow, smelling those familiar farm smells, the fear lessoning and the anger rising every time I left the safe nest of my saddle. I still to this very day do not know truly why this went on for as long as it did. My father had an uncanny diligence about proving his point. It was of utmost importance, so maybe we soldiered on because he wanted to prove to me and my mom this was what needed to happen, and by sheer longevity, his point would be proven.

A funny thing happened as we continued. I can remember so vividly a change in my thinking and a determination rising from the depths of my spirit. It was a shifting inside of myself, akin to physically turning my insides out. A maturing shift that I did not recognize. I can still remember looking at the trees as I was riding in a direction facing away from my parents. My gaze fixed on their deep green depth, I remember wondering what it would feel like if Nail sprouted wings and we flew into the trees, deep into the forest where we would no longer be able to hear the loud bang of his deep voice, "JUMP." We would be safe in that lush tree line, maybe I should just kick her hard and shake the reins, beckoning her to ride hard and fast. But each time I faltered, my eyes would meet the ground. I would swallow back the dread and let go and jump. And every time my body left the saddle, the fall felt easier and easier.

Standing, shifting, falling…standing, shifting, falling.

Looking back on that moment, I know now, on that shift, it was a form of acceptance. Acceptance of the fear. Acceptance of less than ideal circumstances. Acceptance of pain. Acceptance of trust in myself. Acceptance of letting go. Acceptance of something I could not change.

And as it turns out, Acceptance had a best friend with her on this faithless day on the farm. Her name was Confidence, and she and I were formally introduced. She sat beside me in that saddle and whispered her reassurance in my ear before every tumble to the Earth. I was earning her respect and the right to have her ride in the saddle with me. She would help me muster up the courage to fling myself from the safe, secure spot on the back of my horse and fall to the ground with me.

She would then stand with me and resituate herself right beside me on the saddle with Acceptance, reconfirming any doubts that lingered. I really liked Confidence. She made me feel invincible and strong, like I could face the back of any animal I needed to and jump right off. She gave me the reassurance I needed to know I could do this as many times as it would take to satisfy my father that I was sufficiently trained.

Little did I know my relationship with Confidence would face much larger tests than horses. Our relationship would be one of the most fickle and fleeting that I would ever know. It would be one that I would have to fight hard to keep as I grew into a young lady, a woman, and finally a Single Mom.

Before we leave the farm, I want to share with you that I remember my mom saying to my dad, "She will never want to ride a horse again." But I did ride again, at the very next opportunity. However, I never encountered the need to jump off a horse, nor do I ever intend to again.

My relationship with Confidence

Looking back on it now, I can clearly identify those roller coaster ups and downs and all the moments I have struggled with Self-Esteem and Confidence over the years. There have been many times I was able to "fake it until I make it." Then there have been others where confidence left me high and dry, nowhere to be found, and the outcome from those moments were crippling.

These instances range from sprouting boobs faster than anyone else in the fifth grade, and having other girls mock and pick on me because my chest wasn't flat like theirs, to not having the confidence early in my career to ask for the pay I felt I deserved. On the surface, they were not really big events.

Let's face it. Most of us will experience some form of childhood scarring. Kids can be so forward and blunt without meaning to cause long term damage. But the taunting I encountered around the size of my breasts would give me body insecurity issues and diminished self-confidence for years to come.

Not having a high value of self-worth in myself as it related to my job was another ball of wax. This pattern of devaluing myself showed in other areas of my life as well, not exclusively related to a paycheck. In relationships, friendships, in conversations with others, casual ones like the baby sitter or the cashier at a grocery store.

I had a tendency to view myself through a more critical lens, like what I had to say wasn't important or I needed to rush to not take up too much of the person corresponding with me because what I had to say wasn't worth their time. I think to some degree we are all guilty of this. Women especially. We seemingly come out of the womb with this preconceived notion that we are here to be caretakers and nurturers of others, roles which seem to naturally come with connotations of lesser value. It is insanity.

There are few instances, however, that can match how my self-worth, confidence, and internal value system suffered when I became a Single Mom. It is safe to say this was one of the biggest threats to my confidence I have experienced in all my life. While our experiences are all unique, I think it is important for me to share mine to help your understand where I started before we jump into the tools and tips you can use as a recovery mission for confidence building. The ugly truth is I started at the very bottom of the barrel. A cold, hard, empty barrel that had bounced around before coming to a sudden halt, leaving me in a daze of fear, confusion, and curiosity over how my story would play out.

If you look at the statistics around Single Moms, the data is staggering. According to an article written by The Atlantic, in 2015 it was estimated there were twelve million single parent households in the world, and of those, 80% were headed by single mothers. That math puts us just south of ten million single moms world-wide. This demographic is more likely than any of the others to fall below the poverty line.

A couple of compounding factors that hold these women under the poverty line are inadequate child support and low levels of education, which severely limit job choices for a single mother. Not to mention they often are the sole in-person provider for the child, so they have to miss work for dentist and doctor appointments or if the child is ill and unable to attend school or daycare.

I might not have known these particular statistics when I became a Single Mother, but I did know as a general stereo type the outlook was dim. The day I became a Single Mom I was making just over minimum wage with only a high school diploma, and had a mortgage to pay with plenty of other bills to add to the list. I knew child support was not an option for me, so right out of the Single Mom gate, I felt like the odds were stacked firmly against me.

At this point, if I had been statistically categorized, I would have been thrown onto the side of a pie chart with a group of women who most likely needed government assistance just to feed her kids and provide basic amenities.

This realization was coupled with the fact that my marriage had just fallen apart. Eleven years of my life, my identity, quite literally dissipated. All in a moment of decisions. I was now saddled with the prospect of taking on this new identity that felt like a blow to my life's plans and ambitions.

My hope was depleted, my mental well-being was called into question, and my Confidence was nowhere to be found.

Shining a light in dark places

The helplessness swallowed me whole, taking me deep into its belly, swimming in a cesspool of lost dreams. In the early days of my divorce, when the kids would spend time with their dad, my depression was all I had. It was like my new-found best friend. Laying with me on the couch, in my bed, cold water in the bathtub, unable to move, numbed and scared with no clear direction which way to go next.

I have heard people refer to divorce like a death, and I think that is a fair comparison. I mean, it is different in that a physical person is not dying, however a relationship is dying. Even though my relationship had been deteriorating for some time, the person that I was in the relationship was alive and well. This is how I had come to know myself" "I am so and so's mom, or fill in the blank's daughter in law, aunt or wife." I rarely ever introduced myself as just me. I had wrapped my entire existence into a title that represented the life of another being. This realization felt like the hardest loss to me, because I had no idea who I was when standing on my own two feet.

I am unsure how much time I spent wallowing in this void of loss of self, but I am certain it wasn't as long as it felt. Hopelessness has a cruel way of feeling timeless, like you are lost in an abyss of silent space. The truth is—there is sound beyond the silence if you open yourself to hear. And when you open, even if it is just a crack, you are allowing the light to shine in.

Somewhere along the way, I decided to listen for her familiar call, the call of Acceptance. Once I was ready to see her, she appeared as she always had before. Acceptance of pain. Acceptance of trust in myself. Acceptance of letting go. Acceptance of something I could not change. And along with her, just as before, was my Confidence waiting to jump in the saddle with me and take part in the ride.

Like anything else in life, I believe this was a process that is no different for every single person on the planet. We each get to move through our own unique journey. For some, it might be a series of therapy sessions or outward steps that help us move through. For me, it was more of an inward shift where I saw a flicker of hope and grasped it to bring me back to a reality where I understood I had a choice. But here is the thing—without the confidence to entertain that hope, I would not have begun to move and shift through it.

Part of this change includes you being able to identify and listen to the inner dialogue occurring in your mind. We have to make the effort to consciously let the possibility and optimism rise to the surface, and recognize self-doubt and pessimism for what they are and push them down. This takes a lot of practice, but most important it takes a refined level of self-awareness.

To love yourself completely, you must first know yourself

One of the most powerful tools we can pull from our inner arsenal of self is *self-awareness*. This concept and practice is defined as a very clear perception of ones' personality, strengths, weaknesses, motivations, and your thoughts, just to name a few. Self-Awareness is also action-oriented It is the bringing awareness and intention to the examination of yourself, which is not always an easy task.

I believe to find your best self and reach the upper limit of your potential, it is essential to practice a high level of self-awareness. But we are going to start small here. I had a teacher once tell me that to eat the elephant, you take one bite at a time. So, our intentions will focus very specifically on the thoughts in our minds.

Regardless of where you are in your journey, if you just became a single mom or you have been in the thick of it for some time, it is likely you have shifted to a form of survival mode. Survival is a natural reaction, as we are just trying to make it through day to day and survive what comes our way. Our brains have a tendency to shift and come from a place of block and tackle, which makes us hold little regard for how we might be thinking or reacting to a situation. This is where self-awareness can get lost if we are not careful.

Let's think of Self-Awareness as the co-pilot to Survival. She can help ensure your energy is not misguided. Like most of the tools and habits we will learn in this book, it only takes practice to put them to work for you. The other really great part is everything you need you already have.

It is like you are carrying around a tool bag on your person. We are just going to rummage through it a bit, dust off some tools, and totally refine and rework others.

Today we will be practicing self-awareness by looking for negative inner dialogue patterns in our thoughts. One of the most common things we do is to doubt ourselves inwardly. Self-doubt is tricky and can take on many forms: judgement of others, second-guessing a comment or action, being in a situation where you are not sure of the answer, impostor syndrome, and others. If it makes you feel unsure, like you could have/should have done it or said it better, that is self-doubt.

Step One: Recognize It

Once we have identified the self-doubt, what do we do with it? This is where we get to practice asking the hard questions: Why do we feel that way? How can we feel differently? Let's boil it down—at this point, you need only ask yourself two words: *why* and *how*.

The Why: Take a step away from the situation mentally. Close your eyes and imagine when you were a kid blowing bubbles on your lawn. Remember how those bubbles would reflect the light, purples and pinks, as they rose to the sun? Now take one of those bubbles, and for a moment, imagine this situation is in it. Separate the situation from who you are. Once you are holding the situation away from you, it becomes easier to create reasoning in the spaces in between yourself and the situation. Ask yourself a series of questions.

What is it about this situation that makes you create these feelings?

Why do you think you are feeling this way?

Are you personalizing something that wasn't meant to hurt you?

Are you telling yourself a story that is rooted in habit rather than in truth?

Give yourself the grace here to answer each of these with as much honesty as you can gather. Be gentle as you allow these truths to wash over you. It might not feel good, but you have to uncover the root of what is growing this weed of self-doubt if you want to eliminate it.

The How: I am going to be brutally honest. The *how* is not sexy and pretty. It is not something we can wrap in a bow and blame on other circumstances. We are going to learn to own our *how*. What are the words that come to mind as you think about how this makes you feel?

Did it make you feel as if you were not enough? Not intelligent enough, attractive enough, good enough, not quick enough?

These thought patterns are all rooted very deeply in our ego. The chances are whatever you were feeling at the time is closely associated and tied to your ego, which is totally normal and can even be healthy. However, it is important to realize this because your ego is only part of you; it isn't the whole you. Just giving yourself the space to acknowledge how a situation made you feel and understanding it doesn't define you is powerful in and of itself.

You may come up with an overabundance of reasons you feel the way you do, and that is okay. At this point the question is a bit rhetorical. What we want to do successfully is ask the question of ourselves.

Providing the moment of separation between ourselves and the situation helps us to remember we are not that situation, at all. Start practicing now, and remember *why* and *how* each time you do this. You will be teaching your mind to pause and separate.

Make a Choice

We are going to talk a lot about making choices in this book. A lot of the self-doubt that we contend with is our inability to choose to reframe the situation in a different manner. We allow the situation to become boss, and it, along with all the self-doubt, run havoc in our mind, drumming so loudly in our ears that we can't hear or entertain anything else.

If you do not learn anything else from my words and experience, please hear me now and learn this. Making a choice is your power; it belongs to no one but you. You hold the power within you to choose how you are going to react to any situation that you encounter. You must learn to be in control of making these choices.

Once we have learned to separate ourselves from a situation, to pause, reflect, and ask the How and the Why, we are at a place where a choice must be made. What are we going to do with this situation that is not defining who we are? We are going to choose to learn something from it; we are going to make a choice to reflect on it and learn.

Let me acknowledge every situation is different, and you might already experience that voice telling you in your mind, "Yeah, but my situation is different," or "My situation is worse," or, I love this one, "My situation happened to me when I was young," as if there is more validity in the way you feel because you have been carrying it longer.

This is where I will call bullshit on you and say reread the How and the Why. You are not your situation, and this is a good place to implement that practice. My experience is for sure going to be a different flavor of Single Momism than yours. We have to shine a spotlight on what is common, and in this particular scope, it is the choices we decide to make.

Now that we are sitting with our How and our Why, we have to choose what to do with them. We first need to recognize that making a choice doesn't always mean action. It is likely that your choice could be to acknowledge and reflect, meaning you have done the work to separate, now you want to think about the situation before you let it go. This is a great approach, as long as you are intentional in the space you hold for that reflection and do not let the reflection become a cover for you to continue to stew and brew. If you need that time, then choose to take it. Just remember to continue to hold the situation in the pretty bubble outside o yourself.

In the event you are ready to take action, the course you travel is not going to be cookie cutter. Making a choice to act is powerful and, please note, not always tangible. Your action could be that you are going to choose to release said situation altogether. Take a pin, pop that bubble and forget it, lick the wounds to your ego, and move on. This takes a lot of practice, but I promise you—it is an option.

Action for you could look like an apology or an acknowledgement of something you did to contribute to the situation. When you start to self-reflect, you bring some big players into the game. Vulnerability is one of them. When allowing yourself to be vulnerable, with your inner voice replacing that projection of others with a reflection of yourself, all things begin to shift. Ask yourself a hard question. What could you have done differently? The answer may be nothing, but get yourself in the habit of asking that question.

When action involves another person, you have to make a choice to understand you are only in control of you. Perhaps your action means ending a relationship with an acquaintance or your participation in something. When your choice involves others, remind yourself you are only responsible for what you choose to do, say, think, and feel. Others get to decide how they react. We are all grown-ups here.

The Ego is your BFF

When we talk about Confidence, we have to bring Ego to the conversation in a positive light, too. We need to learn to regard our ego as the kid within that never quite grows up. Left unattended, it can be the reason you want to pull your hair out, but when managed and loved it can be your best ally. We have explored and learned to accept that a lot of how we feel and react is driven by ego. And guess what? That is perfectly okay; it is a part of the human psyche.

So how do you tame this feared beast and make it work for you in a positive light? You will likely get tired of me saying this, but the first step to most of the tools and principles in this book begin with acknowledgement. How can you possibly put your Ego, or anything else for that matter, to work for you if you are not willing to acknowledge its existence?

Here is the thing—your Ego knows what is up. She is like that friend who will never ever tell you what you want to hear, but rather, smack her gum, roll her eyes at you, and tell you if you are being a shitty person.

Let's get one thing perfectly straight here. You can't bullshit your Ego, people. Got it? Once you can get real with her, let's also give her the credit she is due.

The Ego craves things like control, superiority, and self-centeredness, just to name a few. We are striving to become self-aware women so we can level up and be the best version of ourselves possible, right? Then clearly, these are not the things we are looking for our Ego to bring to the table. However, we must be aware of them and practice identifying them when they come up. You must ask the hard question and understand why or what in a situation triggered you to feel the need to bring those attributes out.

If there was a specific person or event to point to, then great—you know how to arm yourself the next time you are around this person or in the situation. However, if the trigger is within yourself, you will need to do some reflection on why this is a problem for you.

I have a tendency to fall prey to some of the negative Ego behaviors. No matter how aware I am of them, there are certain people who seem to draw them out of me every time I am around them. So you know what I do? I choose not to be around them when practical, and the other times, I limit my direct interaction with them.

Our Ego is also powerful in other ways, too. It is almost like one of those relationships where you choose to take the good with the bad. I sincerely believe one will not be able to rise to meet the highest version of themselves without understanding the power of Egoism. Let's explore the good that our Ego brings to the equation.

First and foremost, your Ego will help you understand and appreciate who you are and how you differ from the world around you. Society in general puts a lot of pressures on us, especially Single Moms, to subscribe to a predetermined definition of who we are. It makes people in general feel more comfortable to draw nice, tidy boxes around groups of individuals and say, "Oh, you fit in this box, I understand what I can expect of you."

Ego can help us establish a great sense of who we are and what we have to offer the world. If we didn't have some inkling inside to be different, to be better, to be our own person, then the world would be a lot less interesting.

For a woman who understand and accepts who she is will be able to exploit herself interests in a way that promotes her unique persona. She will understand that while other people are different from her in many ways, she can use her understanding to promote growth and benefit in a plethora of ways. What makes us different is what makes us strong, remember this.

A second benefit a well-balanced Ego brings us is heightened self-awareness. Yes, here it is again. That lofty little jewel, when left unexplored, can fly under the radar. Your ego can help you dig this jewel out.

When we open ourselves to seeing why we do the things we do, we stand in an optimum place of power. If you can reflect on why you have particular thoughts, reactions, and emotional responses in your daily life, then you can change patterns.

For example, women are habitual people pleasers. Am I right? We overextend and commit to things that would be a far reach to get done even if we did have a clear schedule. That's one thing a Single Mom never has—a clear schedule. Nonetheless, we say yes to our boss when asked if we can cover that shift, even though there is a mountain of laundry waiting for us at home that we promised ourselves we would do tonight. We say, "Sure, why not?" when the soccer coach asks if we can bring snacks after the game because Suzi-Q's mom is just too busy to stop. We say, "Okay, I am here" when a friend calls and needs consoling, even when we planned to binge on Handmaid's Tale because the kids are finally at their dad's on a weeknight.

When you develop a keen sense of self-awareness, you will understand vividly what you need to operate at your fully embodied highest self. Not only will you understand it, but you will begin to put it into action. The next time you are asked to do something that will tip your responsibility scale, the idea of putting yourself first will be top of your mind, and in turn, you will be more apt to manage your response with a kind, "I would love to, but" response.

Overview

This chapter is very near and dear to my heart for many reasons, but mostly because I know that without my confidence in check, I wouldn't be the best version of myself. I want the same for you. It is so vitally important to your continued success and well-being. It is hard to know exactly how to wrap this chapter up. I mean, we could go on and on about tips and tools to practice confidence. But I subscribe to the idea of less is more, and if you really want to make an effort to change and improve something, you should set out with keeping it as simple as possible.

So, as you start to put these tools into practice for yourself, be sure to take notice of the effect they have in all areas of your life. Remember, you are not your situation, no matter how good, bad, ideal, or not ideal. Everything that is happening to you is temporary. The only permanence is you and your attitude about how you choose to walk through it. Walk with confidence, babe.

Tool #2: Going Beyond What Is Expected

I am a lover of kitchens, and not in the "I want to decorate them with cute little farm pig figurines" kind of way. I just know that some of the best and deepest embedded memories happen in the kitchen. When I reflect on those years living at home after my own mom became a single mother, the memories always seem to gravitate to our kitchen. They are entrenched, they are vivid, and they are felt.

 When my dad left, it seemed that my mom lived in the kitchen. You know that period post-divorce when all your routines and patterns swiftly change? Everything that surrounds you is now different, even the items on your weekly grocery list. I know that for my mom, the kitchen was her warmly familiar place within the constant whirlwind of change. We always knew we could find her busy in the kitchen. She'd be talking away on the phone with friends, or sitting in front of a pile of paper-work accumulated from our schools, or preparing meals with concentrated focus, and it was there where nothing else in the world touched her.

The meal preparation stands out for a few reasons. One, because I was a kid of the eighties. While we had fast food, it wasn't a staple in homes like it is in the present day. You'd expect to be able to count on one hand in a single year the amount of times you were able to eat at Burger King or McDonald's, and most of those trips were tied to a very special occasion, like a birthday party. Our parents and grandparents were super resourceful. They grew their own food in their gardens, created new meals from scratch, and cooked them. During summer break, I clearly remember my mom cooking three square meals per day, like clockwork.

The second reason my mom in the kitchen is so burned in my memory is because the conventional act of simply preparing our food, after becoming a single mom, now had an edge of anxiety tied to it. Whenever we'd return home from a trip to the store, I can remember her carefully portioning out the meat. She stared it down intensely. It was as though if she focused hard enough, or made the right wish, it would magically multiply.

I specifically remember one instance when we had gone to get groceries and my mom purchased a pack of ground beef. It couldn't have been more than a single pound. She wrapped it with saran wrap and made four or five squares of wrap on the counter. As I put away the dry goods, I watched her trying to get exactly equal measures of meat out of those squares. I pretended not to notice.

It would be many years before I would be able to have any point of relation to what she must have been experiencing in that moment with the hamburger meat. It wasn't until I became a single mother myself that I could understand. Meat is one of the most expensive items you can buy, and she had been trying to stretch it and make it go as far as it possibly could to feed us.

I now understand that having enough food was a concern in the back of her mind, always. Her mind was always concerned with having enough of everything, particularly food. She'd tell us to take only two pieces of this, or one of that while fixing our plates. Food scarcity was real back then, and is still a huge issue for single moms today.

My mom never let the fear of not being able to feed us win. She stepped up and took solid action. When she needed to, she re-entered the workforce with zero experience and a hopeful heart, having never worked for an actual wage in all her adult life. She leveraged what she could using relationships, and ended up serving food and assisting with tray cleanup in our elementary school's sweaty, stuffy cafeteria. In awe, I watched her dig deep to find the hidden opportunity and golden ticket of the non-glamorous situation. It was in that school cafeteria where she learned enough about nutrition and meal planning to leverage the experience into something far larger. After a couple of years, she landed a job at a local group home for girls as a food nutritionist, where she was offered more pay, more benefits, and more opportunity. I was proud.

But what would have happened if my mom hadn't seen the job in the cafeteria as an opportunity? Herein lies a problem, when we see these things only as they are instead of choosing to see them as they could be. It takes work, intention, and focus to stretch beyond the initial surface of a situation and create opportunity.

My mom chose to focus on more than just her responsibility to serve food to hundreds of kids each day. She broadened her interest while expressing her strong desire to grow to the manager. Then she naturally began to involve herself in the planning of that food service, developing a keen understanding of the specific criteria those meals had to meet. This experience, along with a stellar recommendation from her boss, gave her all the ammunition she needed to qualify for the job at the group home. This happened because she had gone beyond what was expected of her job.

You see, this is where the pot of gold awaits under the rainbow. Those treasures will remain unearthed if you don't pick up the shovel and dig them out. A situation might not be the most ideal or what you'd hoped, but you can still transform it into something great if you give yourself the opportunity to see it as such. I believe you can make gold out of anything if you look at it right. But first, you have to be willing to see.

Let's take ten people, at random, hand them a piece of paper, and ask them to draw a house with trees and sunshine in the backdrop. Nine of the ten will give you just that. But there will be that one person who adds the clouds, a rainbow, a fence around the house, a pleasant stick-people family, a dog, and even a cat! I mean…they nail it! Now, when you pick up the ten sheets of paper, which one will draw your attention most? It's not just because there is more to look at, but deep down you feel like they've earned the right to have you gaze at their picture a bit longer in exchange and respect for extra effort that was given.

You might feel like you are already using this tool, and there is no possible way you can do more than what you are doing now. I mean, you are a single mom juggling it all, right? You may be thinking to yourself, "No, girl, we ain't going there," or "This doesn't apply to me," or "You don't know my situation." If you had any type of thought that resembled these, then this chapter and tool is more for you than the ladies who are actually open to the idea. How can you possibly do more? Stay with me and let's explore that idea.

The Busy Badge

One of the first things we must touch on here is the concept of busyness being sexy. Our culture has taken the idea of being busy and magnified it in such a way that when someone asks how you are doing, your first tendency is to tell them about the glory of all you have going on, or even worse—you drape the answer "so busy" with a deep sigh, as though that somehow justifies it.

I am going to introduce a, perhaps radical, idea here. I am willing to bet that if you have come this far in my book, then you are a believer and changemaker, operating and conducting your life directly from the heart. And even if you're not making an active change right now, you deeply believe that you can and will help to make a better world and a different way of thinking in both how we humans exist and how we treat each other. Even more importantly, you can demonstrate for your children how this can be done, day in and day out in everything you do, share, and touch.

One of the easiest ways we can do this is to change the narrative from the inside out. We must truly look within and train ourselves to go against that typical grain and refuse to let what we do, how much we do, and the many tasks and lists we have define who we are and how we are as people. It is not our output, but what radiates from within, that matters.

This overworked, overstressed, overloaded culture has sadly become habitual. So, how do you break a bad habit? You stop breathing life into it. You stop giving it your energy and your time, and you put a huge, intentional halt to the pattern. So today, when someone asks how you are doing, I want you to stop what you're doing, turn your body and your feet squarely toward them, look them in the eye, and directly answer them. This will do two beautiful things. First, it will grab their total attention and you will both be fully present. This, in itself, is huge, because as a society we very rarely take the time to give a sincere answer to this type of question!

In fact, the very question itself has even become somewhat second nature, even reduced to the point of just a break from an awkward silence. However, we can do our part to change it. We can stand still, face that person, and answer with honesty. This is where a shift happens, sending ripples of change through the universe. It may be small, but it is impactful. And when you respond with that honesty, remember that you are not your day or your task list, or the amount of hours you've participated in activities, but instead you are a very alive human being sharing a real moment with another real soul. This is a moment where you don't identify yourself with outside circumstances, but tap into the fire and water and earth and air within.

Remember this is a two-part exercise. You've just commanded that person's full attention and have given more thought and sincerity to their question than I'm certain anyone has in quite awhile. And the best part? This tiny yet powerful practice will naturally spread into all other areas and evolve more and more. When we consciously work to change the definition of how we think of ourselves in relation to the time and effort we put into the world, everything becomes a bit sweeter and deeper. So, now it's time to reciprocate. Hold your posture firmly toward them and maintain contact so you can fully see the person in front of you while asking them the question, "How are you doing today?"

Remember—we are not busy. We are actually little humans floating around on this massive ball of water and dirt with billions of other like-minded humans, all chosen to take this incredible ride in space. So, rather than identifying and accepting ourselves as merely "busy," let's self-identify with something far larger and a heck of a lot sexier.

Shooting Star

Remember in grade school that game where if you got the most challenging words right on the spelling test and exceeded the standard 100 grade, your teacher would put a golden star on your paper? I loved those stars so much. I was far less concerned with some mundane score than I was with the pretty, sparkling sticker she chose for my paper.

No matter what your current occupation is, you must remember that you always have the ability to create your own opportunity to gain one of those golden stars.

Before my divorce and just after my daughter was born, I worked a hodgepodge of jobs trying to make enough money to avoid the commitment to return to full time work. I longed to stay home with her that first year but also needed a solid income. So, in addition to cleaning houses, I took a job at a dry cleaner working four hours a day.

The job presented was really easy. I would process in and out clothing for customers, organize the clothing that was ready to be picked up, and get the delivery clothing ready to go out for the following day. Most jobs have "other duties assigned," and this was, of course, no different. During those lagging slower times I was expected to iron clothes.

There are a few things you should understand regarding this. First, I am not your stereo-typical "housewife" material. I took home economics during my sophomore year of high school, mostly to appease my grandmother. One of our assignments was to sew an article of clothing. If you want the ultimate test in figuring out whether you are a patient person, try and sew something. If you're able to make it through cutting out the pattern without cussing and crying, then I'm certain you might be more patient than me. It was a disaster for me. When I sewed that damn thing, the crotch was where my knee cap should be and the hems along the top were visibly uneven. It was so bad that my grandmother stripped all the seams out and resewed it herself. I mean, it had already been submitted for a grade, which I am quite certain was a D at best. Again, I'm not your typical housewife.

And, of course, there are other things about me that just do not line up with housewife type material. I belch and I fart, audibly. I have never been much of the girly girl type, so I really never had the need to have perfectly freshly pressed clothing. I am more the "throw it in the dryer for five minutes and call it good" kind of girl.

So, when my boss who was in her mid to late sixties told me she had clothing I needed to iron, I was absolutely appalled. Let's call this lady Ethel; she was wife to the husband who started the business, mother to the son who now ran it, and obviously had a huge amount of pride in what they had built and an established expectation for what the end product should be, particularly the ironed clothing that I did not want to partake in.

The mere look on my face could have easily put her on high alert, but this was where the dry cleaning job, which was once an easy-peasy four hours of my day took a sharp turn for the worse. When I walked into work on that first day post-ironing, Ethel was waiting for me to walk through the door. "You won't be dealing with the customers today," she muttered. "Come with me." My stomach sank to the earth. We walked back in the direction of the ironing board where there, piled in one huge stack were all the clothes I'd ironed the day prior. She grabbed the article of clothing on the very top. "These are unacceptable, so you will start here and iron these clothes, then you will iron those on the rack behind you." For context, I would estimate it was easily easy seventy-five to one hundred articles of clothing.

She'd periodically come to check my progress as the morning progressed. I had hung the items that were done, and my success rate was about 25% in her inspection process. "No, this will not do," she'd exclaim, ripping it off the hanger and throwing it back onto the pile. I was so quietly frustrated that I may have cursed old Ethel under my breath. In hindsight, I realize I was frustrated with myself. So, what did I do after my four-hour shift of ironing? I went home and ironed some more.

That's right. I took every last button-down shirt and pair of slacks out of the closets, threw them on the table, and got straight to work with new determination. I'll also add that I didn't even have an ironing board, and am not really sure why I didn't go buy one. I just used that kitchen table and got busy.

The following day when I walked in, Ethel was ready for me again, walking me back to my familiar mound of clothing that she'd inspected the day before. "Get going," she instructed. "I will take care of the front of the store." It was obvious to me that she was growing increasingly annoyed. But I was beginning to understand how to do it and improving fast. She definitely noticed. I mean, my success rate with her might have creep up to 60%.

Here comes the game changing, shooting star moment: I mentioned to her that I had been practicing ironing. Her face was visibly surprised, and even touched! "You've been practicing?"

It was obvious that I was doing a better job, and the sheer fact that I had been practicing ironing for a dry cleaner that was paying me minimum wage was probably a big deal to her as a business owner.

I had gone above and beyond. Now, I didn't realize at the time that this would happen, but it shifted the entire dynamic of our relationship. She was immediately more open to help me and show me tricks and tips. She even taught me how to sew a button back on a shirt, something else I am fairly certain my home economics teacher tried to teach me.

The point is this—I was working at a dry cleaner, through a temp agency, making minimum wage which was $7/hour at the time, and was able to set myself apart and earn that shooting star. I went from almost being fired, even though she never said it I could feel it was imminent, to less than a week later being given a dollar an hour raise. No, I am not making this up. I actually got a raise. I was floored.

I could have easily become angry, directing my frustration at Ethel, but I redirected and figured out a way to make the best of my situation. I needed that job, I was going to be there anyway, so why not shoot for the stars? You can hold yourself to a high standard no matter what the job or task is that you are doing.

If you look hard enough at your current situation, no matter your profession, you can identify an opportunity to earn a shooting star. Are you having a hard time with a co-worker? Give them a compliment or offer to do something on a Friday afternoon to cover them so they can leave early. Maybe your boss is a total jerk and is making your forty-hour work week a living hell? Make the opportunity to ask how his/her weekend was or how their child's soccer game went. Most of the time to earn that shooting star, you don't have to necessarily do anything. On the contrary, you just have to show that you take an interest in the person.

It has been my experience that most people in general, particularly negative or difficult to please people, just want to be seen. They want to be seen and they need to be heard. When you see them or when you hear them, you are creating a space that will allow them to connect with you on a level that is elevated. That is the shooting star.

Ethel may or may not have believed that I was ironing at home, because my ironing game was never up to her standard, but I saw her and acknowledged how important it was to her. I was able to demonstrate to her that I recognized her expectation and wanted to do my best to meet or exceed it. There are times in life where if you want to improve your situation, you need to focus your attention on how you can improve others. Here is where you will find most of your shooting star moments.

You can always go beyond what is expected of you. That is right —I said always. Every situation is ripe with opportunity because there is no one individual, boss or otherwise, who has the mental capacity to identify all the little things and direct you to do them. This is one of the things that is so very special about being a human being. We all are born with personal gifts, tendencies that set us apart from one another. When we come together, even in small groups, our personal attributes become a part of a larger collective, but we must make the effort to put them out there to have others recognize the value.

Are you going beyond?

Let's talk about work first. I can tell you there is nothing that burns me more than hearing someone say, "He/She didn't tell me to do that." Or another good one, "He/She didn't say that would be under my scope of responsibility." Let's be honest and call these lines of thinking what they are—lazy cop-outs. At the end of the day, if you have to put that much effort into considering or thinking about what you were not asked or told to do, then you have entirely too much free time on your hands. To begin, let's bring awareness to the situation. Stay with me here because I think you will find the effort is 99% mental and 1% physical.

I want you to ask, "Self—how do I feel about doing more than is expected of me at work?"

Categorize your reaction by identifying with one of the following three choices:

1. There is no way I can do more. I feel as if I am running a marathon everyday already.
2. My job limits me to certain tasks. I am not able to do other things.
3. Why would I do more? I already do more and no one appreciates it.

Number One

If you answered number one, odds are you have been in your job or your specific role for some time now. You feel everyday another challenge presents itself, and that challenge is on top of or in addition to the already existing mound of responsibility you have accumulated since being in your job. So, what can you do? I mean, at this point you are pretty much stuck in this cycle, right?

Wrong!

For one, if you have been in a specific role in your company for more than two years, it is time to ask for a change of scope. If you work at any company of size, your Human Resources Department likely has a growth strategy in place for employees. Ask for a meeting with your HR manager and explore that option. You may be tempted to say to yourself that your company wouldn't be able to do it without you. I promise they can. Be proactive and show your interest in broadening your value within the company by learning more.

If you are in a job that is not rotatable, for example—an executive assistant, you can request to take responsibility in another department. Look, I know this sounds counter intuitive. You just answered with number 1 and are overloaded as is. Just stay with me. Request to job shadow with a department for a day and be on the lookout for something that interests you. And make an offer to take it on for them, even if it is a short-term project. If they decline your request, then job shadow another group. There is someone in your organization who will be willing to offload work to you. Most importantly, you have just broken the cycle of monotony.

Now how do you manage this extra work or new role? We have to retrain ourselves in this realm first, and you can start practicing it right now.

Make an effort to slow everything down. Slow. It. Down. Everything—your thoughts, you list of to-do's and massive effort to multitask, your speech, your actions, all the things. These may be minutes of your life that you are exchanging for a wage to make a living, but they are still your minutes. Go slow and be present with them. To do this, you first have to make yourself aware and identify when you are not being present and intentional. When you catch yourself, and you will, redirect your energy into being slow. I literally want you to move as if you are in quicksand, taking deep breaths for an eight-count along the way.

I used to do everything so fast—walk, talk, and move, and I still do. The difference now is mentally, I am sure I am maintaining a good balance and I am making a conscious effort to move quickly, i.e., I am managing the tasks rather than allowing them to manage me.

A few years ago, I listened to a podcast about how to receive people with your body language when you speak to them, how the busy culture in which we live promotes multitasking when we speak with others, and how this can make the person feel devalued. We try to speak and keep walking, or answer a question as we quickly pass by rather than taking thirty seconds to stand still and answer.

I had to have an honest moment of reflection. I knew I had a tendency to do this, not only with the people I worked with, but even with my kids at home. "Hey kid," as I walked by their room, laundry in hand, going to get hamburger meat out of the freezer to defrost and start a pot of water boiling to make tea. "Did you have a good day at school?" or "How was your day?" which was typically met with an exasperated "fine" or "good." I would roll my eyes and think to myself, *Really? Is that all you have to say to me?*

The truth is I wasn't receiving their response. I was asking as a formality. If I wanted to hear what they had to say, I needed to show them I was open. If I wanted to honestly hear about my co-worker's weekend, or at the very least show her I was interested, then I needed to stop and show her I was ready to receive what she had to tell me. So, I implemented an action I now do every time I am speaking to someone. I turn my feet toward them, which by default turns my body to face them, and I am still while they speak. I do not look at my watch or fidget with my phone. I am intentional in listening to what they have to say.

You have to practice this same type of intention with yourself. Slow yourself down. Most of what you are rushing to do is against a self-imposed timeline.

Aristotle once said, "We are what we repeatedly do." We typically see these quotes in reference to the great, admirable things, however, when Aristotle laid this truth down, he was also talking about the not so sexy things, like being a busybody. We have to recognize we have the ability to impact this and that our actions are what is going to change it. To reteach your brain, you will have to be consistent and persistent in practicing this new approach. You are developing a new habit, and more importantly, replacing it with one that is not serving you.

It is no different than when a child learning to play a guitar. Every day the child picks up the guitar, strums the strings to hear the rhythm, and tries several combinations until his fingers work together to bring the ear magic to life. This doesn't happen on day one, and rarely does it happen on day sixty-one. But each day the paths and neurons in the brain are reformed and reworked to know how to make the sounds until it becomes effortless. We are adaptive and flexible beings, but change is only successful if we put in the effort and time to manifest the desired result.

You must also be brave enough to ask yourself: Am I doing the right things? I know your immediate reaction is "Yes, of course I am," but we want to dig deeper. How many of the responsibilities you currently maintain were provided by your supervisor in a formal job description or verbal discussion? And how many have come up to bridge a gap, solve a problem, or just to do something that wasn't capable of getting done timely? Write down all the daily tasks you currently perform. Beside each one, indicate if it is something you have been asked by an authority figure to do. Anything that was not a directive handed to you—I want you to get rid of it. Give it a couple of weeks and see if anyone notices. You may be surprised to find this task you feel is imperative is not on the radar of anyone else in the company.

Doing the right things doesn't just apply to the tasks you are doing but can also apply to how you spend your time at work. Are you on your phone looking at Facebook or Instagram because you don't drink coffee and you are not chatting over doughnuts like everyone else so you spend your extra time scrolling? Stop it. Today. Put your phone in your desk and do not get it out until lunch time and/or until all the top things that are on the priority list are completed for the day. Procrastination can be a lead cause of making us feel our tasks are larger than we are. Staying ahead of them can boost your confidence and bring a feeling of relief by being ahead of the game.

Number Two

If you answered number two, then you most likely are in a job where your direct labor is part of a larger process. Perhaps you are assigned certain functions that do not allow for some of the freedoms we have discussed with a desk job. You perceive you are paid to maintain a certain responsibility or function and that is it, right? Nothing else matters so long as you do "x," right?

Wrong!

Let's flip the script and examine how simple this can be. We will take a person who works in a factory, on the floor, doing production type work on an assembly line. How can this person possibly do more than is expected?

For starters, show up on time for your shift. Being on time is a way to show respect, not only for your individual job but also for the company. You may be a cog of a much bigger wheel, but you signed up for this. Take pride in what you do and show up on time or even early. This demonstrates you are dependable without a single word being spoken.

Also, be diligent in your break and lunch times. If you get fifteen minutes twice a day, then take fifteen minutes. Do not be the person who everyone knows stretches their time into a run to the bathroom, stop by the vending machine, another to talk on the phone, and it turns into your boss having to track you down. This doesn't accomplish anything helpful for you. It makes you appear like a child who is incapable of managing themselves and their time.

As a side note, I am also a stickler on this in my personal life. I have been late my fair share of times, but for the most part I make a concerted effort to be early or on time, always. I feel it is one of the most simple forms of respect we can show each other—"Hey friend, I respect your time" or "Hey friend, I did what I said I was going to do." These are the messages that are communicated, even if not verbally. We all know that person who everyone worries about if they do not show up five minutes early to a function. You will hear whispers of concern, such as "Sally is never late. I hope everything is all right." Be like Sally. Be someone who your circle of people regards as a sister of her word. Be on time.

Grab a broom. Yes, you read that right. Grab a broom. I have worked in and around production work long enough to know these machines and robots we praise and depend on for 90% of the mechanical devices we use in our lives sometimes break. When they do, downtime is created. Do you look at this as an opportunity to grab your cell phone and check how many likes your latest Instagram post received, or do you reach for the broom? Look, the broom is theoretical here. The point is you offer to do something that is needed during the downtime. Maybe it is sweeping around your work area, or maybe it is picking up around someone else's station while you ask about their day. See if there are any boxes that need to be broken down. I mean, come on, folks, you know your work. Anyone with a little effort can identify things that need to be done. You have to be looking for it and ready to create an opportunity to go beyond the call of duty.

If you don't see anything to do, perhaps ask your manager. "Hey, Manager, what can I do to help while we are down?" This is a last resort, but still a viable option. I am always a fan of being the person who can find something to do on her own, as I generally am capable of self-managing in most situations. But if I am in a situation where I am unsure, then I will ask the question. So, don't stand there with your finger up your rear end. Go ask what you can do to be productive and possibly take the load off someone else.

Number Three

If you answered with this response: Why would you do more, no one appreciates it? We are going to break this down into two separate parts and address each independently.

Why would you do more? There are several reasons. Let's start with the effort you bring to a situation is a representation of the value you bring. This is an element of raising your own self-value through your actions. When you stretch yourself beyond your own perceived limitations, you will increase your own perception of worth.

No one appreciates it. How could you possibly know what others appreciate? This is a version of a copout that keeps you from having to own your own hesitation to actually going above and beyond. Here is the thing—even if someone tells you they appreciate your contribution, if you allow these types of narratives to seep in you will never believe it. Are you really willing to base your value and worth on whether someone may or may not appreciate you? No, you are not, because if you were, you wouldn't be reading this book.

Perception is QUEEN

As women, we are super aware of how the world perceives us, sometimes too much so. For example, there are moms on the PTA who seem to live and breathe bake sales and trivia night. Single Moms are barely able to find enough time in the day to find a clean shirt and brush their teeth, let alone bake a pan of fresh pastry for the Free the Unicorn fundraiser. Am I right? But, nonetheless, we worry.

The point still remains, there is a time and place to worry about how you are perceived and the hours you spend at your job are at the very top of that priority list. You want to be perceived as someone who will go the extra mile to get the job done and done well.

It is not as common as you think. Trust me, the bar is very low in most places. You will see it for yourself if you pay attention. People are filling more and more of their time with mundane tasks, such as taking multiple trips to the copier so they can sneak a peek at their social media page or going for that forty-five minute trip to the break room so they can fill their cups with the four-hour-old stale coffee they do not even plan to drink. We have a lot of first world problems. I am speaking directly to those of us who have the privilege of living in the United States. But this creates environments ripe with opportunity to shine, to be *perceived* as a Rockstar, with very little effort.

One other point to make here. Equally important to being willing, is to ensure you are also perceived as able. In my personal experience, there is nothing worse than trying to work with someone who needs me to hold their hand every step of the way. I would rather just do the thing myself. It is often easier than having to coach them through, which can seem like duplicative effort.

Being able means being someone who can take an idea and trust your expertise enough to figure out how to get it done. Most things are not that complicated, even if you have never done them before. A quick side note here—you will be surprised how many things you can find examples of on YouTube.

I have worked in the finance and accounting industry for over a decade, and Microsoft Excel has been my best friend. I have never had one single class in Excel. I am not an expert. However, I would easily rank myself, on a scale of 1-10, a solid 8.5. The reason for this is because anytime I got stuck or knew there had to be a better way, I took to the old trusty Internet to figure it out. Google and YouTube are some of your very best resources. Use them.

Being able means you are also going to put a foot forward to figure out how to get it done. So, if you ask, be willing to be able to move forward with as much as you possibly can to complete the task yourself. You may just surprise yourself.

Tool #3: Teach The World How To See You

Who did I think I was?

August in Tennessee can be described in an array of adjectives. Ask any native—they can paint an accurate visual. "Today is going to be a scorcher!" or "It is hotter'n blue blazes." Or "It is hot as all get out!" or my all-time favorite, "It is hotter than noon on the Fourth of July." When you grow up in the South, hot, sticky, muggy summers are just something you come to expect and embrace.

But this August day, the heat coupled with the nervous jitters I had in the pit of my stomach were enough to make me feel like I needed to pull the car over and hurl. This would be my first day of school, back to college, a single mom with two kids, at thirty-three years old.

My hands were clammy with nervous sweat as I played over and over in my mind the prospects that were about to occur. The negative chatter in my mind was extra loud on this day.

What would people think of me?
Would I be the oldest in the class?
Who did I think I was?

I just wanted to turn the car around and go home. But the resolve to go back to school was bigger than my self-doubt. I had made the decision to put myself back in school for one reason. I knew that if I wanted to provide a secure future for myself and my kids, this was the only way. So, I kept driving, moving, with nervous resistance, toward the school.

Starting school has never been easy for me. When I was five and started kindergarten, I can remember being equally nervous. Everything in Ms. Suzie's classroom scared me. The cubby where I was to put my nap mat seemed too deep and dark, the shelves of books that I didn't know how to read was as tall as the sky, and the blow up alphabet letter men were like monsters lingering in Ms. Suzie's hidden closest. I never knew which letter would be coming next or where he would be hiding.

For me, a kid of simple beginnings, the introduction to this well organized, Pine-Sol smelling classroom sent me into a tailspin of sensory overload. My first full day of class I was so anxious the entire day that by the time my grandmother came to pick me up, I ran to her as fast as I could with my arms stretched wide. She thought I was coming in for a hug, but she was wrong. I was reaching for the Etienne Aigner purse that was hanging on her shoulder. I grabbed each side and pulling it open as wide as it would go, promptly threw up inside.

Click-Clonk and Support Husbands

So here I was, almost thirty years later, sticky with sweat and wondering if I would make it through my first day without vomiting my guts up. I laughed aloud, looking at my purse in the car seat beside me, sizing it up and imaging how much it could hold. This time there would only be my purse waiting as a faithful holding ground for the remnants of my nervous stomach.

I was alone…all alone. I had been told that for orientation we could bring someone with us. It sounded much like an option that I thought for some reason or another most would opt out of. I mean, we were adults, and this was an adult-oriented study program. Who would bring someone with them, right?

Well, apparently everyone except me.

I walked down the hallway of the massive building. Isn't it strange how places feel so large when they are new to you? It is like when we are kids and everything feels so big, but when we come back to it as adults, it is not nearly as large as we remember. I was having a similar experience in the building, Canton Hall. I could hear the echo of my high-heel shoes with every single step. *Click-clonk.* There was so much empty space between me and the ceiling, *click-clonk,* and hallways that had no end. *Click-clonk.* What in the hell did I think I was doing there?

Finally I found the room where the convocation would take place. I was staring at the plaque on the wall, "Room #08-124," secretly debating whether or not to *click-clonk* back to the safety of my car when I heard footsteps behind me. I turned to lock eyes with a very lovely young lady with a short blonde bob haircut, eyes that twinkled with a smile, and I immediately felt a bit at ease. She must be a student too. Perfect, I wouldn't have to walk in alone. My mind immediately did the calculation…she wasn't quite as old as me. But there was someone behind her, maybe another student. Maybe they were even older.

I reached out my hand to meet hers and we introduced ourselves. "Hi, I am Katie," she said enthusiastically, and went on to tell me she was a student of the program. But the person standing behind her was no student—he was her husband. She patted his arm lightly, explaining with her big smile that he was just there for support. I smiled with understanding. In the back of mind I was aggregating the calculations. *Not only am I older than you, but I also have lost my support husband somewhere along my journey here.*

We wrapped up the simple pleasantries, agreed that we must be in the right place, and turned to enter. I *click-clonked* into the big room behind Katie and her support husband.

Show Up

Inside the room was a large table with chairs all around. There must have been enough seating for fifty people. I immediately try to remember what the program advisor told me about the number of people who would be in my class. You see, this was an organized cohort for adults over the age of twenty-three. The idea of this type of setting was to take people who had more mature experiences and put them together to lean on each other and complete their bachelor's degree in an accelerated manner.

Trying to recall the average class size, I was certain it was no more than twenty-five. My memory was quickly confirmed when I walked closer to the table and could see that every other chair held in it a backpack, and on the table squarely in front of the backpack chairs were name placards.

Examining the room further I could recognize the students clearly. They walked around scanning the table, looking for the right place. The support people were equally easy to distinguish as they were walked behind the students, close to the outside perimeter of the room, trying not to make a fuss or distract their student, and smiling with quick anticipation at the support they were here to provide.

When we were seated, it became abundantly clear to me that of the twenty-three students that made up my new cohort, I was the only one who had come alone. Not everyone was joined by a support husband or wife. There were mothers, fathers, sisters, and brothers. I am sure mine would have been happy to go with me if I had asked. But I didn't. I had chosen to go alone.

Now sitting there in this room of shared excitement and collective anticipation, I had not felt so alone in the time since my divorce. I knew if I were still married, I would have been joined by my husband. This wasn't sad; this was fact.

And there was a great irony in this circumstance. This endeavor, this undertaking, me choosing to go back to school, would be my very own journey to take. I took out my phone and quickly texted my mom, just saying I had made it to orientation and how excited I was. I was really doing it: going to college. Just that act of reaching out to my own support person made me immediately feel better.

The tears that had threatened to sting my eyes quickly changed to exhilaration at sitting among these folks, ready to take a huge step to change my life, my kids' lives, and the circumstances surrounding the stigma of Single Motherhood that we faced.

I listened to the introductions as one by one we took a stand to say hello to our new cohort. As the circle drew closer to my seat, I took a deep breath and a smile <u>involuntarily</u> spread across my lips. Beyond my name, I can't remember exactly what I said. I was so nervous and overrun with emotion by this point that all the words out of my mouth immediately went into a black hole in my mind.

What I do remember is this: I showed up. I showed up without knowing exactly what I was doing. I showed up for my kids because I wanted to make a better life for them. And I showed up for myself because I wanted my degree. I needed to do this, and I knew if I wanted it badly enough, I could do this.

Working and going to school fulltime challenged me in a very different kind of way. It stretched me and made me see that I could do things with my time I never imagined possible. An accelerated program meant we had a shorter amount of time to do the same amount of work. Essentially, what should have been a twenty-four-month program was packed into thirteen months. It meant I had one night of class every single week and hours of homework I had to go through.

Those thirteen months of my life are some of the richest memories I have with me and my kids. Yes, I was busy, we were all busy, because I couldn't possibly do it all. They took on more chores around the house to help. The lawn still had to be mowed, laundry done, floors vacuumed, furniture dusted, and meals cooked. Admittedly, we ate a lot of peanut butter and jelly during this time.

But we did it, and they helped me do it. There were even times the three of us would be doing homework at the kitchen table together, and I would ask them to help me with some of my work. I wanted them to feel a part of the process, too. It was important to me for many reasons. For one, I wanted them to get an idea of what going to college was, and two, I wanted them to understand why I was doing it. I explained to them that if I could get this college degree, then I would qualify for more jobs in the accounting and finance field, and my skillset and experience would be worth more money. They never said it, but I know they got it. Money was tight. It was like a fourth member of our household, pulling up a seat at the kitchen table, and sitting close enough to constantly remind me how fickle it was and how quickly it could run out the front door.

During this time I decided to start taking the kids to church on Sunday. I had never been particularly religious, but my best friend was. She also was a single mom, and invited us to go. The kids, of course, loved the social element. They got to go to Sunday School and eat ice cream. And more times than not, after church, we would go out to eat with my friend and her kids. But beyond just the social aspects, I think they started to latch on to some of the practices as well, like prayer.

I was standing at the kitchen sink one night doing dishes when I felt something wet underneath the bottom edge of the cabinet. After a quick investigation, I figured out the pipe under the sink had sprung a leak. This was when just days before we had a plumbing issue in our main bathroom and had to call a repair man. I will never forget the look on my daughter's face. She was seven years old at the time, when I stood from pulling all the cleaning supplies from the cabinet and shaking my head in total disbelief. She said, "Hey Mom, I don't think our PRAYs are working. Our house is breaking."

All I could do was laugh at this point. I agreed with her. We must be doing something wrong.

But in reality, life as a single mom is hard. It is hard without piling on top a responsibility like school. But it can be done. Let me say that to you again: **It can be done**. Whatever it is you want to do. We have a tendency to talk ourselves out of even trying because the thought of all the things that will go wrong beat us down. We cower, we hide, and we become bitter and regretful because we didn't chase our dreams.

There is no reason for this to be your reality. Believe me, hear me, trust me. You can do anything you want to do.

In May of 2013, I graduated with my bachelor's degree, and my kids were there to watch me walk across that stage. After the ceremony, I hugged them both and through tears, told them, "We did it. I could have never done it without the two of you." It was true. They were a huge part of my motivation to keep moving, keep balancing all the things, and keep succeeding.

While everything I just told you is super true, it is also important for me to tell you it was hard.

It took me showing up every single day as someone I had not yet become. Someone who believed in herself. Someone who knew she was worthy too. Someone who knew she could be the first in her family tree to achieve a college degree. Someone who believed she could do this, even though the prospect of the task seemed larger than what my life could support.

I believed if I showed up and went through the motions, then I would fall into my natural place. I simply refused to let the world, our society, or statistics tell me who I was going to be. I believed if I showed up in the world as who I wanted to be, then in turn I could teach the world who I was. I could in fact, *teach* the world how to see me. I just had to show up and step into it.

Teaching the World

We have all been through a version of what I described with my experience of going back to school. Being thrown in a complete tail spin, off our game. It could be something as simple as speaking up in a group of people where we might not be comfortable. Most of us have been there. We are in a room filled with people who speak the same language we do, but there is something different in the thoughts they choose to express. The words seem to roll off their tongue effortlessly, and the vocabulary is fresh and polished like a beaming, brand-new red sports car.

And you, here you sit with the voice in your head compiling all the reasons you are not enough, why you shouldn't be here, or why you will remain silent. How could your words, ideas, and thoughts ever compare to these brilliant people who are allowing you to share their space?

Right? Can you relate? Have you been there, slouching lower in your seat, hoping no one asks you a question or engages you for your opinion?

I certainly know I have, more times that I can count. It still happens to me if I am not careful to be intentional and drive my thoughts in a different direction. I want to share with you some of my most practical tips and tricks to change that behavior and start to manage those situations differently.

1. Slow. Your. Roll.

Not just any roll here, we are slowing down the words that roll off your tongue, your speech. When we are apprehensive it comes through in our body language and our words. It is a terrible feeling when we find ourselves in a situation where we do not feel confident or just feel we need to hurry through a thought because we are wasting someone's time with our nonsense.

The reason doesn't matter, you need to understand this rule first. All situations apply:

Personal

Professional

Friendships

Relationships

Engaging with that stranger in the doctor's office who is complimenting you on your purse.

Every. Single. Situation.

For the next five days, every time you open your mouth to speak to someone other than yourself, I want you to think these words:

"This is my time to speak. This is my time to be heard. This is my time."

Practice saying this aloud right now.

"This is my time to speak. This is my time to be heard. This is my time."

I want to be clear about one thing. This is not a mantra, meaning this is not something I want you to practice chanting to yourself in front of the mirror before you brush your teeth and go to bed.

This is an intentional exercise to make you aware of the space you are demanding as you speak the words you have to say. You are stepping into your space in the world, between you and your audience, and you are allowing yourself the grace to speak each syllable with intention.

"This is my time to speak. This is my time to be heard. This is my time."

Try this, starting today, and please journal how it makes you feel afterward. Reflection helps us reinforce the practice and make it that much stronger when we implement it the next time.

2. Ask Questions...All the Questions

This is something we hear very early in our lives: "There are no dumb questions!" As a child, we are fueled by questions, like our curiosity is a life force running on an endless battery of wonder.

But somewhere along the way, we start to worry about the way others will perceive our questions, such as "Will I look stupid if I ask?" or "Should I know that already?" Or my personal favorite, "What if I am the only person (sitting in this room of 107 people) who doesn't know that?"

Whatever will *they* think of me?!?!

Here is the thing—they won't. Even more likely, they will be glad someone dared to speak up and ask.

Let's just play this out for a second and pretend those 107 folks sitting in the imaginary room *do* know the answer to the question. Which is worse, you sitting there building up anxious energy in your body, missing out on the knowledge or clarity you deserve, or taking a chance on what these people think and not getting the piece of knowledge you crave? Most of them will not even matter in your life in five months, five days, or hell, even five minutes)

When we deny ourselves the opportunity to speak up, we are training our brains to think we are not deserving of the opportunity to be heard. We are conditioning our soul to push down that child-like curiosity that makes us unique and fascinating in who we are.

Please do not make the mistake of thinking this doesn't apply to you. I promise it does. When you start to pay attention, I am convinced you will see it for yourself, if you don't already.

Starting today, I want you to find five situations in your day where you identify the opportunity to ask a question. Intentionally, you are going to actively look for questions to ask.

Before you start to build reasons in your mind why this will not work for you, let me give you some examples of opportunities to ask questions:

You are in the grocery store and you see a lady sporting a pair of yoga pants that are super cute and likely super cozy. Approach her, pay her a compliment, then ask the question, "Where did you get them?"

You are in a meeting at work, and the feeling in the air is tense and urgent. People are talking fast, throwing around ideas and planning how to best get the task ahead completed. Raise your hand and ask for clarity on a point that was said *or* propose a different solution. "I have a question. What exactly is the deadline on this project? It isn't clear to me?" Or you can say, "I have a question. Who is requesting this information, and do we know what it will be used for?"

You are waiting in the dentist's office to get your teeth cleaned and some unsuspecting stranger is thumbing through a copy of People from 2013. Here is your chance. "Hi there, I am curious. What is the best restaurant you have eaten at lately? I want to take my husband to dinner for a surprise, and want to go somewhere we have never been."

The point here is to give your creativity the chance to have a voice, to speak up, to be heard, to be recognized. Not by the others in the room with you, but by *you*, darling. Look for an opportunity to ask the questions, and you will awaken a part of your brain that forgot it was alive and in existence.

Remember, five situations, for the next five days, and you need to journal about these or write each one down at the end of the day. Be sure to note how it made you feel when you raised your hand or stepped into a stranger's space to insert yourself. Most importantly, how did you feel after doing this?

3. Dream Out Loud

One of the biggest things that happen to us when we become Single Moms is we forget we are allowed to have dreams and aspirations, too. We do not do this intentionally, of course, it is just sheer cause and effect.

We get busy juggling the lunch planning, the kids' soccer schedules, the grocery list, getting the yard work done, making sure to get the oil changed, play dates and sleepovers, and buying that perfect gift for our sister for her birthday so she knows we still remember she exists. All the things that take up time and space in our days and within our minds.

And we forget to make time to dream. Or we are just too damn tired to make the time.

You have to remember that this stage is just a step on your life journey and path. While yes, it is critically important to make sure your children are bathed, fed, and raised to be good humans, it is also important to keep the Dreamer that lives inside of you well, too.

Right now I want you to write down five things that you have wanted to do in the past or want to do in the future. What are the first five things that come to mind? Write those things down on paper. Those are dreams that are closest to your heart and soul.

I am going to do this exercise to give you examples. Ready... Set... Go:

1. I would like to write a book.
2. I want to live in a different place, state, area for an extended period of time.

3. I want to create a circle of friends, a network that shares my interests.
4. I want to camp more often and be close to a body of water so I can drink my coffee and hear nature.
5. I want to be an entrepreneur, building a company that leaves an impact on lives.

Those were authentically the things that came to my mind at the moment. You can see how broad and wildly different they are, but they are there, close to the center of who I am.

Now the work. These five things are going to be your focus over the next five days. Number 1 is up for Day #1—you are going to ponder on this all day. I want you to journal about it, doodle on paper and draw about it, talk to friends over coffee about it, get on the internet and research it, join a meet up where it is discussed and plan to attend within the next thirty days.

You get the point. Each dream is going to get the opportunity to be your close companion for a day.

You owe yourself this. You deserve the right to dream.

At the end of the five days, I want you to reflect on what you learned about each of these dreams. Some may be more viable than others, some may require more planning, or some might be related to a phase you are going through at the moment.

Some might just be things you are going to carry with you into the future to transform into reality.

The objective here is not to determine if or when these dreams will come true. But rather to give yourself space and permission to dream again.

This is for you

This chapter is honestly one you can have fun with. As promised, the steps are easy, implementable, and actionable. They are also flexible. The point is to begin to step into who you want to be with courage and a resolute belief in yourself and see that you are 100% capable of doing anything you want to do. You just have to have enough confidence (there is that tricky word again) in yourself to show up and be in the situation. Each time you do this, the times that follow will become easier.

Tool #4: Remember Who You Are

Walls

If there was one thing that made me feel claustrophobic in my early years as a single mother, it was walls. Walls we honestly didn't want to be inside of, like those germ-infested barriers of the McDonald's Playland. Walls that created some unspoken expectation about how children should act while inside of them. We have all found ourselves, at one time or another, feeling enclosed by walls echoing the loud sounds of children playing, their shrieking voices bouncing around the tight enclosures. I much preferred my kids to play outdoors, to be in parks, ponds, or anywhere they can yell, run, wrestle, stomp in the mud, and simply be free in their young, wild expression.

So, it is no surprise that when I first became a single mom, I found myself outside more often than not. My ex and I agreed on joint custody, which meant half of my time would be spent alone and outside, crying. Outside there were no walls to witness my grief and overwhelming fears that stemmed from not knowing who I actually was without my kids beside me. Those waves of pain often had me on my knees. Outside there were no empty chairs at the kitchen table mocking me. No empty couches or beds. The absence of little bodies hurting my heart as they were sitting in new chairs, in a new home with a new family structure that didn't include me. Those walls surrounding me became a constant reminder of a life I no longer held to fill the space they created.

It was a strange place, my house and those walls, in the early days of being a single mom. I found it very strange to be alone in my house, like even the spiders that lived in the webs of the dark corners of the ceilings were watching, mocking, and wondering what in the hell I was doing there. After one pass through the bedrooms to pick up toys, clothes, and random unmatched socks from the floor, the spaces would stay clean and tidy for days after.

I would question myself, "Is this normal?" "What in the world do I do with myself inside these walls if I don't have tidying and mothering to do?" If I didn't have anyone to focus on, was I supposed to focus on myself?

As I pondered these questions, I would inevitably find myself staring at those goddamn walls.

It is not only the physical walls we have to contend with when we become single moms, but also the figurative ones society paints around us in efforts to know what to do with us. The confinements are not only applicable to single parents. Collectively, we as a society have a tendency to paint people into walled boxes, both inwardly and outwardly. It makes us feel more comfortable when we can familiarize someone and relate them immediately into a group or classification.

But the parameters of the single parent, single mom box gave me a feeling of claustrophobia, stifling my breath, saddling me with an overwhelming sense of hopelessness, fear, and sense of desperation. When we become single mothers, not only do we have to align ourselves with a new existence, but we also have to dig deep inside ourselves to remember who we are beyond a title or a box that the world tells us to quietly sit inside of. The truth of the matter is, no matter what box the world tries to paint us into, we always have the ability within ourselves to pick up the eraser and our own paint brush and start to draw the picture we decide for ourselves. But first, we must remember, beyond our situation, beyond the circumstances, at the root of it all, we have to remember who we are.

Journey

The first weekend I came home to an empty house was the first weekend I was on my own while the kids were at their dad's house. I remember clearly the week leading up to that Friday: The kids would be picked up at school and at daycare and dropped back at each place the following Monday morning. I did not have to arrange it, I did not have to make sure anyone knew about it, all I had to do was surrender to it and accept it was happening.

Really, was this such a terrible thing?

I mean, I had a full weekend ahead of me with zero responsibility. I could do anything I wanted to do. So, all week my mind explored the options. I would rent a movie on Friday night, eat dinner in the living room in front of the TV, maybe even have a glass or two of cheap wine. Saturday I would visit friends, maybe go out dancing, and Sunday I would take a warm bath and read a good book, you know, have a self-care day.

As we all know, the best intended plans do not always come to fruition. Mine started to go off the rails with a small decision to make a left turn as opposed to a right.

You see, the place I worked was just down the road from my son's school. When I got off work that Friday evening, I debated on intentionally going the other direction, a right turn, so I didn't pass the school. However, my curiosity wouldn't let me. I had to see if I could catch a glimpse of him being picked up. I knew it was close to the time his dad would be getting him. What would be the harm in me driving by to see if I could catch a quick look?

And so, I turned from the parking lot, pointing my car in the direction of the school. This was a day in late January, one where the world is still, cold, and hard. The trees are bare and the grass is stagnant; a swirl of browns and greys seemed to hang in the sky, reminding you the daylight is short and the nights are long. They are even longer when you are alone.

There were no cars in the pickup lane and the parking lot was open and empty. A wave of disappointment hit me square in the chest. I realized right away it wasn't curiosity that drove me on this path; it was habit and a lingering sense of responsibility. This was the way I was supposed to drive my car. I was supposed to make that left turn out of my work parking lot and head in the direction of my kid, my son. One of the two pieces of life that existed on this earth that reminded me I was real, I was here for a reason, I was needed.

But there would be no evidence of this to be found there. Maybe I was too late or maybe I was too early. I still to this day do not know. All I do know is I sat at that 4-way stop, blinker clicking to indicate my right turn, sitting, staring at the school blankly, willing his car to pull up, willing my son to step outside so I could see him be picked up, willing any sign of life to show itself around the school. I needed to be reminded that I had a purpose, I was needed. But nothing but an empty parking lot and a naked oak tree stared back at me. That was when the first teardrop fell from my eye, the first contribution to an ocean of tears.

I didn't make it to the video store for that movie rental, nor did I buy that cheap bottle of wine. I don't recall unloading my car or even walking in my house. All I remember is finding myself some time later on the kitchen floor, my back against the corner of the bar, knees held tight to my chest. I hadn't turned the lights on in the house, so when the sky turned to black, so did everything around me. There I continued to sit, continued to cry, continued to wonder exactly what to do with myself, comforted only by the feeling of the solid cabinet behind me. It was the most subtle security as I pressed my back harder into it, as if to ground myself, and continued to cry.

At some point I found my way to bed and woke the next morning with the fog of a cry hangover balancing above my brow. My simple calculated weekend events had shifted, so I didn't give a second thought to changing my Sunday bath to Saturday morning. The hot water gave me a sense of calm and comfort that I needed. I lay still with a hot washrag on my face, hoping to relieve some of the puffiness under my eyes. The water seemed to dissipate the effects from the night before and the light coming through the windows was a reminder of life, of rebirth.

The light was a sign of strength and of purpose in its own right. Much like me, much like my life, much like my reason for being here, there was a light burning deep inside. I was here for an entire array of reasons, one of which was for my kids, but not solely for them. In that moment I realized I had made it through that first night, and I would make it through the next. I released the water from the tub, dressed, and headed to that place where I could find my solace waiting. Where no walls, no constraints, no boundaries existed. I needed to get outside.

I sat on my patio for a bit, drinking my coffee and watching the squirrels chase each other round and round the trunk of the huge maple tree in my backyard. My next door neighbor had told me one day, while I was working in the flower pots in the back yard, it was a sugar maple. That tree and these squirrels were my solace. I must have drunk an entire pot of coffee that morning. Sitting, watching, waiting, and wondering when and if another wave of tears would come.

That is when I decided to take a drive, to nowhere in particular. I just wanted to open the moonroof to feel the cool air and ride.

And so, for hours and hours, I drove.

The fresh air that tunneled through the car with the sound of songs I knew every word to blasting on the radio was the perfect simplistic therapy that day. I was reminded what it felt like to play whatever music I wanted at full volume on the speakers as opposed to tolerating whatever teenny bop music my kids were into at the moment. I will admit, that was a nice change. I had forgotten how nice it was to have control of the radio. I mean, seriously, the things we do for our kids. I do not think we realize how much of ourselves we give away when we become mothers. It is the little things and the big things all combined, creating this vortex of changes that are so slight we don't see until we are forced to take notice.

The clouds were fluffy in the cold sky on this winter day, but my heart was warm with memory. Memory of how I loved the open road ahead of me and the sight of the mountains in the background. Memory of a feeling of freedom, nowhere to be, nothing to do, and no one waiting for me. Memory of smiles and simplistic daydreaming, feeding my overactive imagination. Memory and the sensation of myself, the foundation of who I was flooding back and filling my chest.

This Saturday drive was more than a road trip to nowhere. It was the beginning of my journey back to myself. Every second that passed I uncovered more satisfaction in being alone in that car. With the wind in my hair and cool breeze on my skin, I started to feel a sense of awareness of self, an inner strength buried deep inside, twisting and turning, fighting to surface. I could feel it rising slowly, a reminder of who I used to be and how that spirit had slowly merged with who I was today.

I was a lot of things on the surface: an ex-wife, a single parent, a divorcèe, and so many undesirable titles the world doesn't present to you when you are a little girl reading books filled with stories of white horses, handsome princes, and castles that meet the clouds in the sky. Oh no, these are the taboo titles we women sometimes find on the other side of a not so "storybook ending" of our own journeys.

And while it is true, the world would recognize me as these objectionable titles, it was also true at the root of each one of them was *me*. And the *me* that I know would and could make it through this time in my life. I would and could encourage that nudge inside to continue to rise to the surface, reminding me who I was, both with and without my kids. I would and could move forward with my own dreams and desires because at the end of the day, no matter what circumstance I find myself in, this is my life, my shot, my chance. And I would not and could not take the finality of that feeling lightly.

Like a Virgin

I had the ultimate girl crush on Madonna growing up. Remember, I am a kid of the 80's, in a time when Teen Beat and MTV were our exclusive entertainment in an Aqua Net=fueled fluorescent leg warmer wearing existence. I was hell bent and determined that when I started driving, I would have a personalized license plate that read: MADNNA1. My mom rolled her eyes and laughed at me, but my fixation continued to grow. Ultimately, I collected enough fold out posters from various magazines to completely cover the walls of my side of the bedroom. I shared a room with my sister, and I threatened to chop the heads off every Barbie she owned if she touched my posters or messed with my music.

As much as I loved Madonna's music then, and still to this very day know every word to her early albums by heart, I do not believe it was her songs alone that appealed to me. I mean, I didn't even know what a virgin was, and I didn't care. I wanted to be brave and unruffled like this person. I wanted to emulate a certain level of authority in my reality. I can remember the first time I saw the

Material Girl video. I was seven or eight years old and was captivated by the way that the "lady" on the screen commanded her space. I was accustomed to seeing women in dresses and pearls act conservative, living in accordance with the unspoken "lady-like" standards that are passed down by generations. I am sure you know them: always crossing your legs when wearing a dress, do not run, jump or skip when wearing a dress, do not tuck your hair behind your ears when wearing a dress, do not bite your nails when wearing a dress, and for the love of God, do not fall into the arms of men when wearing a dress.

Madonna obviously did not subscribe to these rules. She made the rules, and she completely and thoroughly owned whatever space she was in. The confidence seemed to drip from her pores. My child mind would not be able to understand what it was telling me for years to come. I now understand I was captivated by the combination of her ability to own who she was and command the space that surrounded her.

I was fascinated by this demanding exterior that challenged every half-hearted belief I had known in my short life about being a female. The contradiction was playing out right in front of my eyes This woman and her confidence, her undeniable right to belong, her courage to dress in whatever she wanted, the poised words that seamlessly rolled off her tongue, all of these things were a beacon of light and hope that even at a very young age introduced to me the notion that I did not have to conform to this preordained existence of sugar and spice and everything nice. I was perfectly capable of defining my own being and deciding who I was going to be.

Stop Shrinking

As I began to pull myself out of my single mother shell and remember who I was, I felt a nudge and reminder outside myself to do the same. Women, single mother or not, have so many wonderful gifts to bring to the world. But so many times we do not see it that way. Maybe we never did, or maybe it is the overwhelming weight of our circumstances that anchor us so far down we forget.

Working in corporate America for many years, I have seen so many women walk into a conference room full of people, primarily men, and physically shrink and reduce themselves by drawing their shoulders in, bending their knees a bit, and walking almost tiptoe around the room to find a seat.

Cheryl Sandberg famously touted in her book, *Lean In*, that women should take their seat at the table. There is a reason that phrase resonated and washed like a wave through the community of business women. Many of us have been in situations, be it corporate or something similar, where we felt we didn't belong at the proverbial table. I have read so many articles and books over the years that explore the logic behind this behavior, and I believe they are all on point. In summary they will tell you: We are women, so naturally our role is to support others and be sure everyone around us has what they need. However, I feel that we hide behind these façades a bit. It's like we reach a point of understanding then internalize that thought of, "Okay, now I understand why I do this, I am female after all, it must be normal." Then the next time there is an opportunity, we pull up a seat at the table, but inside we still do not feel like we belong.

The point is, you can sit at any damn table you like but if you don't believe you belong there, then no one is going to notice you anyway. You have to own your right, your space, your belonging and scoot your chair up to that damn table and put your elbows on it and ask, "What is on the agenda for today?"

This is not only for my business, ladies, you can be a stay at home mom, a baker, a florist, a seamstress, an event planner, you can be Strawberry freaking Shortcake, the point is when you encounter a situation where that little voice in the back of your head questions if you should be there, you need to sit up straight, stick that chest out, and own your space. You have just as much right as any person on Earth to be where you are any moment in time. Believe it.

How you hold yourself matters. you need to save the slouch for the couch. When standing and engaging with someone, plant your feet firmly on the floor and hold your shoulders square and strong. Think of yourself as an oak tree (I read this years ago and have envisioned it so many times) and do not shrink yourself. The oak tree reaches for the edges of its width, strong and fierce to the sky. Embrace that posture. If you are sitting, put your back against the chair and position yourself in a manner that is comfortable.

Again, do not shrink. I will share one thing I picked up many years ago that I am super aware of in others: I want to see your hands when seated, visible at all times. I think that shows you are open and willing to put it all on the table. I have no science to provide for this tip, however it seems to me that I am more forthcoming with the person I am engaged in conversation with when I practice this.

Look Me in the Eye

When I was a kid, we rode the bus to school. If you were driving a straight shot, from driveway to driveway it was about a fifteen minute drive. But we rode the school bus which is not a point A to point B type ride, so our daily commute was more like an hour, both in the mornings and afternoons. We had a lot of time to pass, so we played weird games like a staring contests. I am not suggesting you stare someone in the eyes so long you have streams of tears running down your cheeks, but I do think there is something to holding good eye contact.

I feel like this goes hand in hand with the aforementioned. When you are present in a situation, you can engage without ever speaking a single word if you maintain eye contact. The aversion to maintain eye contact is typically associated with being shy or not having a sense of confidence. But the good news is, just like riding a bike, with intention and practice, you can improve this skill. Like most of the techniques we cover in this book, it all begins with awareness.

The very next person you come into contact with—give it a try. While speaking, make eye contact 50% of the time. This will relieve some of the pressure on you and allow you to look away at natural intervals during the conversation. When listening however, you should be actively engaged and hold the gaze a bit longer. Increase your connection to 70%. And remember, Rome wasn't built in a day. Just putting this into practice is a huge step in the right direction. Every time you try, you will improve your eye contact game.

Walk your Walk

Early one morning when I was no more than two or three, I was walking down the hall to my parents' bedroom. My mom and I were the only ones home; my dad was still at work, finishing his night shift. When I entered her room, she sat up straight in bed and said, "Oh wow, I thought it was your dad home early." I have always had a hard stepping walk. I have left a job before and one of the people wrote in my farewell card that they would miss hearing my walk come down the hall in the morning.

Like so many of the other things we cover in this chapter, women (most of us anyway) have the tendency to try to make ourselves small and quiet. This includes doing something as non-trivial as walking.

Lift your gaze. Your target can shift, but avoid looking at your feet. Avoid bouncing your head from side to side; you are not a bobble head doll. Keep your gaze pointed straight, even with an ever evolving target. Make your steps wide and purposeful, as if you are a woman on a mission. Because really, aren't we always? Avoid putting your hands in your pockets; remember, showing the hands is a powerful display of trust and confidence.

The truth of the matter is it is really not so important how you choose to walk. It is more important that when you take steps, even the trivial seemingly unimportant ones, you do so with purpose, courage, and heart.

Hugs over Handshakes

It is no surprise this chapter is the hardest for me to write. I am and have always been a bit of a non-conventional, challenge the status quo kind of girl. However, all the tips I have shared here had to be mentioned because there is something to be said for boldly being comfortable in your own skin. As much as I would love to tell you, "It doesn't matter how you come across to others. Do you, girl," that would be doing you a disservice, because truth is, it does matter. What you choose to do about it is completely up to you, but at a minimum, you need to be aware.

Now we are going to take a hard left. Are you ready? Hold on tight.

I will never forget the first time I was aware of a handshake. Like you, I had heard all the cautions of not letting my wrist be limp, taking a firm grasp, maintaining eye contact as your hand bounces up and down a good three or four times. Here is the thing—it no longer feels real or genuine to me.

As a society, we overcomplicate so many things, and I feel like the art of a good handshake is one of them. People are no longer reaching to shake your hand because they are genuinely glad to meet you. When they take the reach to meet your hand, they are priming themselves for the art of the handshake, and the actual human connection is lost. We are no longer reaching because we are glad to meet the person on the other end of the hand. We are simply moving through the act.

So, opt for a hug instead. To be fair, not every situation that presents itself is going to be appropriate for a hug over a handshake, but there are more than you might realize. Look for these opportunities to present themselves and take advantage. It doesn't even have to be a full-on embrace. Just extend yourself to the person and see what happens.

This accomplishes a couple of things right out of the gate. First, the person feels a genuine connection with you. They have taken the trip into your personal space and lived to tell the tale. Second, it shows you have an interest in the person beyond a surface level introduction. It is as if from the beginning, you have taken this new acquaintance to a deeper level of relationship. Third, it makes you feel at ease with this new person just through the sheer act of the embrace. A hug can make us settle into comfort and feel less nervous quicker than a handshake. Let me add a quick disclaimer here—this is not backed by scientific research or proof. You only have my word here. I have tried it, and I promise you—it works.

Summary

One of my favorite quotes of all times is from Charles Bukowski:

"Can you remember who you were before the world told you who to be?"

Can you?
Close your eyes tight and envision the first memory you have as a kid. Dig deep, see yourself, outside of who you are today, then

force yourself to travel along that timeline, witnessing your growth into the woman you are today.

I am on my swing set, stringy dirty blonde hair flying behind me, dirt on my knees, and always a song on my lips. I was born with a free spirit and the bravery to speak my mind, even when the world suggested I sit down and shut up. I grew into a young lady who loved her family very hard, especially my brother and sister. I terrorized them at times, sure. But I also supported them and made so many good memories with them over the years. I found what I was really good at when I began working as a teenager. I was self-disciplined and a hard worker, and I was good at making money and providing for those around me. I didn't wish to become a mother but when it happened, I was overcome with a love I never knew existed. I dove headfirst into parenthood; it was my primary purpose for so many years. I learned what death felt like when I lost my grandmother on my daughter's first birthday. It wasn't witnessing the dying that was hard. It was watching the death loom and taunt and take her slowly that broke my heart open wide. I have tasted loss of a marriage and a companion, seeing those closest to me shift in and out of my life. I have made new relationships and lost old ones. I have laughed, I have cried, I have grown.

And now I sit here wrapping up this chapter, sharing my story with you. My kids are now twenty-one and sixteen, and I am still most proud of my title as parent. But I also know that I am other things, and I am honored by those other things I get to be. I have traveled quite the long journey to find myself, as you no doubt have done yourself or will get to do. Just remember, that little girl is inside you, where it all began. She is laughing wildly, carefree at the root of all the things you have become, waiting for you to remember her, waiting for you to choose her.

Tool #5: Expand Your Mind

If curiosity killed the cat, creativity gave her life

When my son was three years old and I was still married to his dad, we adopted a cat. She was not quite a year old when we brought her home. The people who had fostered her had named her Roxy. These people had also kept her outside, so Roxy was already accustomed to prowling around and adventuring out on her own. We chose not only to keep the name she had been given, but we also let her keep her adventurous spirit, primarily residing outside.

In those early days, Roxy got everyone's full attention. My son couldn't wait to find her when we got home at the end of the work day. I would watch them while I cooked dinner, running and playing over every inch of the backyard. They were bosom buddies. Instead of a boy and his dog, it was a boy and his cat.

As time passed and yet another member was added to our family, my daughter, we slowly became like one of those picture frame families. You know, the placeholder pictures that are put inside new picture frames. The people that look like your stereotypical middle-class family. They drive a minivan, wave to the neighbors as they pass them on the street, and watch Little House on the Prairie at night over a family-sized bowl of popcorn. The mom speaks with incredulous patience dripping from her voice and the dad towers over the lot of them with his larger than life presence, topped off by his slick, perfectly combed hair. There we were, slowly becoming our own version of the picture frame family with our mortgage, minivan, kids, and pet cat Roxy. But soon enough our picture fell to the earth and shattered.

While my ex and I shared joint custody of the kids after our divorce, I had sole custody of Roxy. I believe that cat knew our picture frame family had crashed and burned and she wasn't sticking around to molder with them. It was nothing for me to go days without seeing her. Maybe it was because she was getting older or maybe she knew the afternoon play sessions were now limited to every other week. I will never know exactly what caused her new inclination to roam. I would think nothing of not seeing her for days at a time.

This drove me to think of her less and less. Or at least that is the excuse I tell myself. How does one forget they have an animal? It must be because they do not see her often enough to remember, right? Wrong. I was preoccupied, and the existence of Roxy was lingering somewhere in the very back of my mind. She was out of sight and out of my mind most of the time. So, there were times I forgot about her completely. I would leave food and water in her bowl that would end up sitting there for days. One night I came home to find an opossum eating her food. After almost having a heart attack at the sight of it, I took her food up and didn't put it back out for days.

This was the start of me forgetting to feed her. Yep, you read that right. I forgot to feed my cat, or more accurately stated, I only fed her or set out food when I actually put eyes on her. And it wasn't that I only remembered to feed her when I put eyes on her, it was more like I only remembered she existed when I put eyes on her. I couldn't relate to that disciplined, well-adjusted woman who used to make sure the food bowl stayed full at all times. Oh, hell no, that woman crashed and burned with the rest of her picture frame family. And in the ashes, this is what was born. Far from a phoenix and far from the perfect little mother and housewife, I wasn't sure who I was anymore. And forgetting to feed the cat was only one sign of exactly how lost I was. Not only had I become this weirdly part grown woman and part mother who didn't know exactly what to do with herself, I had also become one of the most horrible pet owners ever.

But when Roxy did choose to make her appearances, she didn't appear to be malnourished, skinny, or unfed. As a matter of fact, you could clearly see that she was eating. One day I spotted her in the far corner of the backyard, occupied by something on the ground. Pawing, jumping back, pawing, jumping back. I was curious, so I called for her. She turned to acknowledge me and just as abruptly turned back to whatever was holding her attention. But this time her motion was swift and deliberate; play time was clearly over. She went in hard and took something in her mouth. As she turned to come to me, I could see it, unsure of what it was, clearly jetting out both sides of her jaws.

As she approached, the suspect object started to come into view: feathers, stick-like feet, beak—it was a bird. Not a baby bird, but a full grown bird. I was stunned and I must admit, a bit impressed.

You see, cats are survivors by nature, with their animal instincts and relentless drive to survive. Roxy knew something was going down when her picture frame family suddenly dissipated. She sensed something was different and her instinct to survive kicked in. I will never know if she was finding food elsewhere—as much as she roamed, she could have had a second family for all I know—or if she was simply hunting to survive. What I do know is she expanded her own possibilities when she felt her situation begin to shift and change. She expanded her thinking and her reality and made adjustments that would keep her animal instinct satisfied. She was creative inside her situation; she refused to sit there and burn with us. Her curiosity would drive her and her creativity would feed her, and so, she thrived.

We women are much the same with our instincts, but we as humans have more potential to expound upon those dispositions. To do this, however, we first must be willing to accept the simple fact that we can. We must start looking for ways to broaden our minds and our thinking and let the survival instincts flow through us. We must open to the potential, the possibilities, and embrace the creativity to thrive.

"The mind, once expanded to dimensions of larger ideas, never returns to its original size." ~ Oliver Wendell Holmes.

Roxy lived a full sixteen years of life with us and I have since wondered in the years since she passed what would have happened if I had brought her inside. She would have made for a great companion in those early days of me becoming a Single Mom. We could have kept each other company. She would have been the one thing left in the world who still needed and depended on me. We would have both been better for it, right? I am not so sure. Roxy was accustomed to being free. She had expanded her vision beyond that of a lazy and contented house cat. Coming into the house to live with me would have felt like confinement to her and limited her scope of life and creativity. Her mind had been expanded through the sheer experiences of life. She learned to open her mind to possibility and embrace the resourcefulness within herself to live free.

In this chapter we will walk through tips and tools that will help you to expand your mind and broaden the creativity you hold deep inside you. Your instincts are already whispering that you hold the power within. I am confident of this, otherwise you wouldn't be reading this sentence here with me now. Take this with an open mind and heart.

Webster

When I was no more than ten or eleven years old, my grandmother gave me a dictionary. This big red brick of a book would stay with me through middle school and high school, as I would reference it any time I heard a word I had never heard before. At some point, I decided anytime I heard a new word I would use a highlighter to mark it on the page, indicating this mysterious little being was now rested firmly in my brain for future reference.

It is so interesting, if you think about it, to introduce a new word, a new idea, a new place, a new anything to your brain. Your brain—that little computer inside your head that is partners with you to devise every step you take in this life of yours. Each time we learn something new, our brain forms new connections and neurons and makes existing neural pathways stronger or weaker. A neural pathway is essentially the paths that connect one part of the nervous system to another. When something new is introduced, circuits travel along these paths in our brains making connections with other paths along the way.

In the example of a new word, when you read the word, the visual aspect of your brain will latch onto spelling. When you speak the word aloud, the auditory portion of your brain will connect the sound of the word with the spelling of the word, forming a connection along paths. Your brain is dynamic and needs to be stimulated consistently to keep you on your toes.

I will be the first to admit that while I maintained a respectable GPA in grade school, I was never an academic elite. However, I believe I have always held a healthy respect for the availability of knowledge and learning. In today's world, information is literally available to us at the click of button. Actually, we don't have to physically do anything to get the information we seek anymore, as many homes have digital devices in them that are now prompted by no more than the sound of your voice.

There is so much information and education available to us in all sorts of consumable formats. In this chapter, we will explore the ways to actively and passively engage your brain in new ideas and experiences. You will find in many cases it doesn't require a lot of time, money, or effort to do this—only your intention, dedication, and accountability.

Read-Read-Read

One of the most simplistic ways we can expand our mind's new information is to read. The beauty of this is there are no boundaries, no right or wrong information. It is player's preference all the way. If you like to read the sex-dripping romance novels, great. If your genre is blood-dripping horror stories, perfect. If you like to read about adventure, travel, and exploration, right on. Or if you like to read personal development type books, and no doubt you do because you are reading this gem, then you are in luck as you can find books for any area you want to develop. The point is, no matter your preference, you can find a book to meet the desire.

When we read a book, we have to maintain and hold on to information, such as character names, relationships and lineage, plots and sub plots, and more. All of this becomes exercise for your mind, not to mention the adventure of creating the visual of entire scenes.

There are tons of studies that support research that reading helps reduce stress and depression as well. There are so many studies it is hard to quote just one, but the consistent stat that popped up over and over again while doing research on this topic was: Reading can help to reduce stress by up to 68%. Losing yourself in a plotline in a life that is built via your subconscious is a prime way to make you forget about the troubles you have at the current moment. As for depression, the general idea is that reading helps us to empathize and develop a keen sense of self-awareness from an unbiased perspective. These skills will then then be subconsciously applied to our waking life.

One of my favorite quotes from Dr. Seuss is:

"The more that you read, the more things you will know. The more that you learn, the more places you'll go."

It's so simple, yet so true. Knowledge is the one thing you take with you everywhere in this life. No matter what, it can't be taken from you. Relationships, jobs, material items, even your health is fickle, but not the knowledge that you store and retain deep in your mind.

Reading helps you gain knowledge which equips you to deal with challenges that come from day to day living. This is largely because reading will help you experience life vicariously through characters in a novel or principles learned in nonfiction. It is like you can cheat the system and broaden your perspective just by reading words on a page, and the good news is your brain will not know the difference.

A challenge that Single Moms face is having the time to be able to sit down and curl up with a book. Thus here we introduce the beauty of technology and audible versions of books. I will admit when I first jumped on the audio book train, it felt a bit like cheating, as if I was cutting miles off a half-marathon or sneaking a brownie when I was supposed to be on a rigorous eating plan. But after a good five plus years of listening to endless hours of audiobooks, I have found them to sometimes be more empowering and enlightening than reading the text on a page. It is such an efficient use of downtime. Commuting to work, waiting at on kids at practice for soccer, football, volleyball, etc., taking a shower, working out, and cooking dinner are all great examples of times when you can turn on an audiobook.

Meditation

I will be completely transparent on this one. I am very new to meditation and it isn't a practice I used in the thick of my time as a Single Mom. However, even just beginning to scratch the surface, I have seen the differences in my patience and my ability to manage my anxiety levels when I am regularly meditating. And if you find yourself questioning if meditation would work for you or if you would be able to do it, that means you are one of the ones who it would probably benefit the most.

    I found the act of mediation a bit suspect at first. I questioned how sitting in silence for minutes could possibly have any meaningful impact on my day. Then I discovered that some of the people I admire and look up to the most practice meditation daily: Oprah, Lewis Howes, Arianna Huffington, even sports greats like Michael Jordan and Kobe Bryant. So, if you have any doubts about whether it is worth the time, keep those names in mind.

    There are many types of meditation to consider. A couple of the most popular are transcendental and mantra. I do not have an in-depth knowledge of either, but I will say from my experience, these seem to resonate the closest with my personal meditation preferences. I gravitate toward practices that are easy to immerse yourself in with little or no prep work. In my mind, it is easier to understand something I can jump into straight away without having what feels like a job to get prepped. Just try to sit down in pure silence for 5 minutes, put your body in a comfortable, quiet place, and sit with your eyes closed.

As far as what type of meditation will work best for you—my advice is to experiment with a few and try them on to see what fits. The most important thing to remember is not to overthink or overcomplicate this. Just download an app on your phone. There are several good ones that offer a trial period or are free all together. This is my approach to a lot of things when I try them for the first time. Just jump in—the water is fine.

Journal

I struggled with adding this one as a sub-bullet in a chapter because I truly feel I could write an entire chapter just on journaling and how it has impacted my life. Journaling is a powerful tool to provide your subconscious with a voice and a way to speak its truth into reality. When you reflect on your experiences and provide yourself with a platform to express the meaning you perceive, it will allow you to feel thorough and almost do a form of checking yourself. Life management and creative expansion is all wrapped up in one subtle action—writing.

I have journaled my way through a divorce and the fears of starting over and being alone forever. I have journaled on the scarcity and anxiety associated with being a Single Mom and the fear associated with finding myself in a position where I would not be able to provide for my family. I have journaled when I was back on the dating scene and encountered everything from a man who didn't call me back because I owned my own home (small detail—he was thirty-five years old and lived with his parents) to a romantic dinner with a gentleman who proceeded to express his vast disgust for his ex-wife, literally from the time the appetizers hit the table until I was scooping the last of my brownie and ice cream from my dessert plate. Truly, there are things you will discuss with your girlfriends in a way that will make you feel better, and of course if you are in therapy, you can put it all out on the table there. However, they will never feel the same as taking the time to give yourself the intimacy of nothing more than the pen, the paper, and your thoughts.

Write it by hand. There is something more connected and relatable when you put the pen to paper as opposed to a digital outlet. I personally believe the benefits manifest themselves in a deeper, more penetrating way. Clearly, most of us can type faster than we can write and often we prefer to type for this reason alone. Writing forces us to slow down, which is not necessarily a bad thing. When we are in a slower pattern, our focus increases and more thoughts and ideas can have the space to come to the surface. Capture everything that comes out, write it on the page. Often when I am journaling, I will catch myself thinking, "If someone were to read this, they would think I am (fill in the blank)." Resist the urge to allow yourself to engage in judgement journaling. It is you, your paper, and your pen, free to wander safely into the depths of what you desire and how you feel.

This is one that you can literally start today. It is as easy as purchasing a pad of paper and a pen, or something you likely have laying around your home. I recommend dating your entries so you essentially create a timeline of your life events. I have found it very therapeutic to reflect on my experiences and frame of mind during a certain mark in time. We can learn from our own patterns and behavior; additionally we can track our progress and our growth.

If you feel you do not have anything to journal about and you are not able to generate a topic specific to a situation you are experiencing, that is perfectly fine. Ask yourself a few probing questions. How does my heart feel? What is my next big action step? What do I miss most from my childhood? These are a few tried and true go-tos that I have used. It doesn't have to be a huge takeaway, either. Your next big action step might be to finally clean out the refrigerator. Write about it and you will see what comes to the surface, why you have been putting it off and how those competing priorities make you feel. With any luck, you will gain some insight to these patterns and learn how to mitigate them in the future.

The company you keep

It has been said that your potential can be predicted based the sum of the achievements of the five closest friends you keep, therefore, you should make them count. I will be honest, to me that statement has a very profound ring to it; it's super definitive. There's almost a level of finality to it. I am a believer, that just like a bad marriage, you can course correct from any bad relationship and rise above it. But we have to give credence to the fact that the company you keep most certainly has an impact on you and your life's compass.

Think back for a moment to the earliest memory you have of making a friend. What was it that connected you to that person? For some it could be as simple as you happened to be in the same class in elementary school and sit beside each other in lunch. For others it could be along the lines of discovering common interests, such as liking the same music bands or having the same favorite color. Nonetheless, the connection is made and the underlying influence begins to have its effect. Relating to this influence, it is important to also remember these connections could be positive or negative. The trick here is to take a step back and examine any relationship you begin and ensure there are aspects and attributes of that person that mirror the goals you have for yourself.

Take a moment to reflect on your closest friends and ask yourself a few simple questions. How do you feel when you are around them? Do they complain about their situations, portraying themselves as victims of their circumstances? Or on the contrary, are they go-getters who make things happen for themselves? Do you feel motivated after spending time with them? Do you feel they could offer you advice on that one aspect of your life you would like to improve upon?

I will be very honest with you—it took me longer than the other kids to figure this one out.

When I was thinking of going back to school to pursue my bachelor's degree, I was spending a lot of time with a guy we will call Tim. If I were classifying my relationship with Tim on Facebook at that point in time, I would have selected: "it's complicated." Nonetheless, our bond was tight, and man, did we have a lot of fun. You see, Tim owned a Harley and we would plan long weekend trips on that bike on so many of the early weekends when I didn't have the kids. As most of you know, it is a very strange time for a single parent, those first weekends that the kids are with the other parent. You fall a momentary sense of freedom, like "I can turn the TV to whatever channel I like and eat all the Oreos I want without having to share." But there are only so many hours one can sit in front of the tube, and even though I can put away some Oreos, they truly lose that lackluster after a while.

And so we rode. I would sit on the back of that bike and daydream while watching the mountains and clouds as they passed by. If I closed my eyes, it almost felt like I were flying. And Tim was great. He was originally from California, and was a lot older than me. A lot. seventeen years a lot. He was, to this day, one of the most chill and laid back people I have ever met. At that point in my life, I did not have a lot of experience to draw from, so I would listen in awe to stories of his time in California, time spent on the beach and carefree. He also was a nudist. I think this is a crucial fact to adequately portray the full picture of just how free Tim was. It was his carefree, laid back, don't have a care in the world style that attracted me to him, and ultimately, it was the very same attributes that drove me away.

I had been thinking of going back to school even before I got divorced. Education had always been important to me and deep down, I did regret that I didn't follow through with college out of high school. So, it wasn't an entirely new idea to me. it had been dancing around in my mind for months by the time I shared it with Tim.

To be fair, I am not sure what I expected him to say. I am not even sure that I totally considered what his reaction would be at all. I am very decisive person, meaning if I decide I want to do something, I am ready to move on it, and move quickly.

His reaction was more of shock than excitement, and I will never forget the way that felt in my gut. I think I knew this whole complicated arrangement was temporary way before that moment, but there is no doubt this solidified it for me. I do not remember exactly what he said, but it was along the lines of: "Why would you want to do that?" and "You make good money, good enough," and "Why would you want to spend money for an education?"

To be fair to Tim, these are all valid, vetting type questions and I completely understand that school is not for everyone. However, it was for me, for more reasons than just one. The first was I wasn't making a lot of money. As a matter of fact, I was living paycheck to paycheck, and it caused me a lot of stress that I spoke to Tim about often. Not only that, but it was abundantly clear by this point if I wanted to move up in the finance industry, it would require some type of formal education.

There is no doubt in my mind that ultimately Tim would have supported my decision to go back to school, but the undoing of the relationship occurred before he had the chance. I also believe that if we had stayed together, I would not have finished school because it wouldn't have been a priority within the dynamic of the relationship. That is really the point here that I want you to take away.

Influence is everywhere. You can pick up your phone or turn on the television, hell you can even walk out to the mailbox and be influenced by a car driving down the road. But we have to be careful and super intentional on what we are spending our time being influenced by, and most importantly, by whom. Inevitably, the people we surround ourselves with most will have an effect on our thinking, our choices, and consequently on our behavior.

Deconstructing Limiting Beliefs, Limited Thinking, and Tomatoes

When I was a kid, both sets of grandparents and one set of my great-grandparents had gardens. Now these were not just any gardens. In my kid eyes, these were massive stretches of earth that offered sweet abundance that I loved to have my kid adventures in every time I visited. I would eat cucumbers, strawberries, grapes, and tomatoes straight off the vine. Yes, without taking them in to wash them...have I mentioned that I was a bit of a tomboy? I am certain I knocked the dirt off or wiped them off on my shirt. Probably not, but it's a nice false reassurance.

One summer in the eighties, the tomatoes came in early, plentiful, and in the most pristine colors of red my young eyes had ever seen. And so, I ate for days in my grandma's garden, as many tomatoes as my belly could handle. One day I must have pushed my limits, or eaten a tomato that by my adult standards should have been washed, and I threw up tomatoes for what felt like an hour. I was so sick that even the thought of a tomato would send me into a hurling fit, turning my innards inside out and chucking my guts up. That day the belief was born—I do not like tomatoes.

Now I am not sure of the exact timeline, but I think I must have been four or five when the Great Summer of the Tomato happened. I can remember being in my early preteen years at a family cookout at the lake where my aunt was preparing everyone's burgers while we played in the water. "Sonya, do you want lettuce, onion, and tomatoes on your burger?". Ad I defiantly answered, in the same tone I had used so many times since my great tomato yarking, "NO TOMATOES!"

I was firmly convinced that tomatoes and all things associated with them were evil and gross. It is really difficult now for me to imagine a time in my life that I didn't like ketchup, but even that I had deemed to be a product of the devil. Several more summers passed and once I was into my teens, I spent time at my aunt's farm. We had taken the four-wheelers up on the mountain for the day, one of my favorite adventures when I was young. We were about four hours in when we found this perfect open patch on the other side of the mountain. It's picturesque in my memory, like the spot you would see a couple choose in a movie for a romantic picnic. We laid out our blankets and out came the picnic baskets from the backs of the ATVs. I was so very hungry that day. I remember it was a cooler summer day and we had been riding for so long…it felt good to sit in the sun and stretch out and feel the grass beneath the weight of my body. I was so caught up in the moment, I didn't even take time to consider what the lunch that was laid beside me must have been. I unwrapped the sandwich and immediately took a bite. It was like heaven. I quite literally swear to this day that sandwich was the best I have ever had in my life.

And so, I chomped it down, every crumb and morsel went down the hatch in no more than a minute. So quickly, in fact that when I had finished, my aunt was still pulling sandwiches from the picnic basket. That was when she realized her mistake, which would ultimately be the undoing of one of the biggest limited beliefs of my young life.

My sandwich, the one that did not have tomatoes on it, was still at the bottom of the picnic basket. She had mistakenly given me one of the sandwiches on top, probably because I was complaining of being hungry. She pulled out the first one she could get her hands on and gave it to me to shut me up.

But by this time, the damage was done, the tomatoes were in my belly, and I had enjoyed every single bite. At first when she told me I had eaten a sandwich with tomatoes on it, I didn't believe her. But at some point, she convinced me to have a bite of one of the others that had tomatoes just to test and see if it tasted the same as what I had just eaten. I was reluctant but ultimately, I complied. And as I bit into that sandwich, the same yummy goodness exploded into my mouth, heaven yet again. And so I did, in fact, like tomatoes. I would no longer be the kid who wouldn't eat a tomato or the girl who didn't like ketchup.

I can still vividly remember that day and how it felt to process this fact about myself that I had adamantly stuck by for a huge part of my childhood. It was not true and the undoing of it rippled through my body and the limiting belief vanished into thin air. It was no longer my truth.

This example, while simple, is an accurate depiction of what so many of us do to ourselves in life. We make a decision about who we are, what we like, and what we can and cannot do in life. We are the artful masters of picking up that pencil and drawing ourselves neatly into a box. To make matters worse, not only do we do it to ourselves, we do it with others as well.

Let's consider for a moment Dorothy in The Wizard of Oz. What do you think would have happened to Dorothy if, rather than opening the door when her house came crashing down on top of the Wicked Witch of the East, she would have merely looked out the peep hole? What if she saw that amazing illuminating light on the other side of the door but decided it was too bright and too scary to step into? Or saw that blazing street of gold, that the audience comes to know as the yellow brick road, but was too afraid to step on it because it wasn't the gravel and dirt she was used to walking on? What about the munchkins? What if she had spied them from the safety of her wind-damaged home and decided they were not her kind of people because they were short and dressed funny, not like the people she was accustomed to spending her time with?

Dorothy's adventure would have been extremely different and extremely limited had she only peered through the peephole rather than stepping to the other side of the door. That is exactly what we do when we make a decision about something and tell ourselves the story over and over in our minds that supports limited thinking and beliefs.

Limiting beliefs keep you from seeing what is possible for yourself, and sadly will prevent you from taking action. The good news is we are only dealing with a mindset here and like all the other goodies we unravel in the book, this one can be changed with a bit of practice. Even better news—you can start right now.

The next time you catch yourself saying things like:
"I do not like…"
"I am not good at …"
"I am not a ….kind of person"
"I couldn't do …."
"I will never have …"

All these initial thoughts coupled with the ideas that complete them are common examples of limiting beliefs. When you identify these, stop immediately to ask yourself five simple questions:

1. Why am I telling myself this?
2. What truth do I have to support this?
3. When did I first become aware of why I think this?
4. Am I going to continue to allow myself to believe this?
5. What do I have in my sphere of influence to change this?

These questions will help you to consider the reality surrounding the belief and understand and identify what is truly your preference versus a belief that is not rooted in truth.

Tool #6: Money and Finances

Fear, Hot Wheels, and Jobs

The Christmas of 2004 was much like its predecessors. it came in hard and fast and no matter how many ways I tried to budget for it, there just never seemed to be enough. Enough—there it is, the elusive, intangible, ideologic, *enough*. We will talk more on this point in a bit—back to 2004. I was sitting on my bedroom floor surrounded by all the tools for wrapping presents and loads of discount paper, no doubt clearance items from the year before, scattered around, so that I could make each $0.97 Hot Wheels I bought as presents for my son distinct in its own way.

    I do not remember exactly, but I would estimate I purchased twelve to fifteen of these little cars and trucks—not because my son was a lover of Hot Wheels, oh no—but to satisfy my own obsession with being able to provide *enough* for him to open. It was during that moment, one of frustration and sadness, judging myself for not being able to give my kids the *enough* that I thought would make their Christmas great, that I got the call that set me on a path that would forever change the trajectory of my life.

If this were a work of fiction, this is where I would likely introduce the ghost of my Grandmother, who just happened to pass away in August 2004. I would continue to tell you that she appeared within a faintness of stardust and luminated butterflies, grabbing my chin and wiping my tears, whispering in a voice that was her very own musical symphony that the phone call I was about to receive was important. I needed to answer, I needed to accept the invitation to interview for this job, and everything would work out in my favor.

But this isn't the way it worked out, because it never is the way it goes when we are faced with a crossroads, right? The truth is I almost did not answer the phone when it rang because I had yet to make it through half of the cars that needed wrapping and it was probably only a matter of minutes before one of the kids burst into the bedroom to see what I was doing. Nonetheless, my curiosity of who might be on the other end got the better of me and I answered the call.

The voice on the other end was familiar and cheery, one that by this point I had known for over 10 years—Paula Reeves. Paula was a staffing agent who also taught a program for High School Seniors called School to Work at our local high school. I was a senior in 1994 and was selected to take her course, that is right, you had to be selected or chosen. I still to this day do not know how or why I was picked, but nonetheless, it was one of the most interesting and memorable parts of my high school experience.

Paula is one of those people who is happy without even trying, much like an elf or a gnome, and joy leaks from her pores. She made quite the impression on me during our time together in the program, providing insight for how things operated in the working world. One of the most impressionable was to make the class do a recorded interview with her. Oh, how I wish I knew where that tape was now. She prepped us for weeks on the types of questions that were standard and a number of responses for each. Not only the Q&A portion of the interview, but also the body language piece, how to set your posture in the seat, what to do with your hands, how to hold eye contact, all the things that are nowhere near the normal tendencies for a senior in high school. Over the course of the six weeks we spent with Paula, I had come to view her as a master of knowledge and insight as it pertained to success in the business world. So it was only natural that when I found myself here a decade later in need of a job, because my then husband had just lost his, and the five to eight houses I was cleaning a week couldn't keep us a float, that I reached out to Paula and her staffing agency to see if she could help me.

    I recognized right away from her energy on the other end of the phone that she was pleased with herself and the reason for the call, and she thought I would be as well. She proceeded, "I know we just placed you at the laundry mat, but honey, there is a reception job at one of the local factories that I just know you will be a perfect fit for. I have already told them I have their girl. When can you interview?"

    Here is the thing—for someone who has experienced financial insecurities, we do not take any job for granted. At this point I had only been at the laundry mat for a tick over a month. How could I possibly leave? I mean, I was just really getting good at ironing as we have already covered in a previous chapter. Not only that, but it was a guaranteed paycheck, while not very much at a minimum wage rate, it was still steady income.

    So, my first reaction was to decline, to refuse to take a chance out of fear and stepping into the abyss of the unknown. I had a sure thing going for me, I was just getting into a grove with my new employer, and was unsure if the receptionist job didn't work out that I would be able to go back. All the doubts and fears rose to the top to show their ugly heads, to whisper in my ear all the reasons why this was a terrible idea. I breathed through their chaos and put each of the opportunities on my imaginary balance scale.

In this case, the weighting factor for each was not what the job offered at the present moment, but what it might offer me in terms of future growth and opportunity. Let's get real and level here for a second. If you think about a laundry mat counter person and a receptionist at face value, when both positions pay exactly the same there is not a lot of distinction.

This is a very critical point to understand. The decision point wasn't around which job I wanted to do for the immediate term. The decision point was completely based on which of the two could give me more leverage in the long term. And this decision was the first of many that I would make in the coming decades that was not solely rooted in the prospect at hand but rather in the runaway that they would afford me to open up opportunity for myself.

So, with reluctance, I answered Paula with an unsure but firm, "Yes, I would like to interview for the position and am available as soon as this afternoon." And as you already know from a previous chapter, I got the job.

I feel like this story is an important component in money management because half the battle we face as Single Moms is understanding that we must always be on the lookout for ways to maximize our earning potential. Money management and awareness, while super important, is only one side of the coin.

Enough

If you are one who cringes in disgust or swells with anxiety at just the sheer mention of the name of this chapter, please know you are not alone. The words money, wealth, and abundance can be trigger words for women in general, but for a Single Mom, we tie all kinds of things to these words. Our ability to provide, our ability to sustain, and our ability to identify our own sense of how much is enough and find our own worth. If we are not careful, we can draw ourselves into a circle of fear that will stifle our creativity and the belief that we, too, can create a life of security and abundance.

I have spent so many days, months, years of my life worrying about money. Not having enough, not being about to provide enough, enough, enough, enough. There is that pesky word, bouncing around like a ping pong ball in the anxious crevasses of my mind. How much is enough, really? Have you ever stopped to consider that maybe being able to buy the store brand bread instead of the off brand once a month is enough? Or ever thought of enough as being able to put your kids in new school clothes even if the majority of them come from second hand stores is enough? Or treating yourself to that mid-range bottle of wine when the kids are with their dad instead of the cheap stuff you normally buy and relishing every single sip—is that enough? Or what about getting creative with the family vacations and taking your kids to a campground that has a pool and making s'mores over the fire—is that enough?

Enough is nothing more than a state of mind. Enough is only what you, in the depths of your heart, your soul, and your mind, decide it to be. Sure, there are plenty of people living with more than you, but there are also plenty of people living with less. Be proud of where you are and what you are providing and give yourself the grace to know that some days will look better than others. Accept that you are doing the best you can and that this world can ask of you.

I beg of you to soften and open yourself to this idea of wealth management. Give yourself grace as you read through the principles presented here and know that the success of this chapter is not rooted in how much money you have. It is rooted in the spirit of what you have is enough and we will walk through the ways you can best make it work for you.

Planning

I believe the management of money and creation of abundance truly comes down to only a few simple elements, all of which we will touch upon in this chapter. There are so many schools of thought on this subject in recent years it seems that everyone has come up with their version of magic steps to wealth generation, creation, and money management. For years I have followed and closely studied these principles and taken away those that have fit and discarded those that did not. I am not going to try to recreate the wheel here by no means. I am, however, going to highlight my version of steps and tips that have worked for me and set you up with the strategies to put them into use immediately.

Dwight Eisenhower once said, "Plans are nothing. Planning is everything."

The art of planning in and of itself opens your mind up to possibility, to hope, to understanding and imagining what is achievable. If you want to make a change or have a tangible result, you have to do the planning. Unless your name is Cinderella, there is no Fairy Godmother coming to wave her magic wand and make money fly around your head, magically whisking away all of your money woes. This step is one of the most fun because it allows you to ask yourself the questions you might not normally take the time or opportunity to ask. Trust me on this one. Grab a notebook and paper and let's get to work. I got you; just trust me.

The 4 Step Easy-Peasy Approach

We are going to break this down into 4 sections: monthly debt definition, income generation, total amount of debt owed, and income generation opportunities. Grab a sheet of notebook paper and write those 4 sections across the top of the page. Now let's go to work.

1. Debt Definition: How much do you have going out each month? Write it all down, every single expense you have during the month, e.g., rent, insurance, car payments, utilities, groceries, child care, entertainment (movies, dining out), clothes, toiletries, cosmetics, nail salon, hair salon, it is all fair game. We are going to quantify these things by monthly expense, even if they do not occur monthly. All expenses that occur once a year should be broken down into a monthly figure (total expense / 12 months), Christmas and birthdays included. Even if you do not know exactly, put it down as a placeholder for now.

2. Income Generation: How much do you have coming in each month? Similar to Step 1, you are going to quantify exactly how much you have coming in. This, of course, includes your paycheck, child support, any side hustle activity, etc. Do not include annual one-offs in this amount, such as tax return or work bonus. Only things that come in on a monthly cadence; it is all fair game. List it on the page.

3. Total Debts Owed: Now for all the monthly expenses you wrote in Step 1, I want you to list the total amount owed for each. For example, if you wrote car payment, how much would it be to pay off your car today? Or if you have a credit card listed, what is the total balance due on that card? Write those figures on the page.

4. Income Generation Opportunity: What are other things you can do to generate income? Do not shut down before you hear me out here. There are things that you can do, even if you feel tapped out, exhausted with no more time to possibly spare. What can you sell? What talent do you have that you can monetize? What expertise do you have that you can offer as a service people need and would be willing to pay for? This is just a prompt to get the juices flowing and capture any low-hanging fruit. We will be pulling some creativity out on this one, so anything goes, even if you are not exactly sure how you will turn it into a money-making opportunity, just simply put it on the page.

Now we are going to do some simple math. Total the numbers you have from Step 1 and do the same for Step 2. Subtract step 2 numbers from step 1, we are going to call this our residual monthly funds. Write that on the page and circle it.

Now once you have completed a first pass at this and you have listed everything down on the page, I want us to dive a bit deeper. Let's review each one of these categories in detail to make sure we have a good representation on which to base our plan.

Debt Definition is a step in the process that is very much like dieting. You know, that single bite of chocolate cake that we sneak in the middle of the night or that spoonful of peanut butter than slides down your throat so quickly it is impossible your body absorbed any of its caloric contribution. The truth is that it does count. We all know but yet we continue to pretend it doesn't, and we deprive ourselves during "normal business hours," doing all the things, checking all the boxes, maintaining our food journals but then wonder at the end of a week why we are not seeing the one to two pounds lost that all the medical journals say we should see. It is because we are not being completely transparent in our process. We are ignoring the mud that gets caught between our toes in those little steps. Small things add up to be very large, impactful things.

It is much the same with our spending habits, and we have come to a point where we need to get real about what we are spending, how much we are spending, and why we are spending it. There tends to be an element of shame associated with spending money, especially when it comes to spending it on ourselves. So clear that pattern, right now, and get super honest with yourself. You will only have success in this process if you are able to paint the picture so you can begin to articulate the path. If you have spent money on it in the last six months more than once per month, then write it down because it belongs on the page. For example, getting your nails done, going to the hair salon, going to the mall for a new pair of jeans, getting a massage. I name these things because they are not what we tend to think of when we think of debt, but guess what? You might not have an amount of money loaned to you for these things, but if you are spending money on them on a semi-regular basis, they are part of your monthly debts. Put them on the page.

Income Generation is a bit more straight forward, the easiest of the steps. Anything you are currently earning money for is listed on the page. These are the earnings you can count on for certain—your salary, court-ordered child support, alimony, etc.

Total Debts Owed are equally straight forward. Ask yourself 2 simple questions:

How much do I owe?
To whom do I owe it?

Income Generation Opportunity is going to require a bit of out of the box thinking for some of us. Chances are if you didn't immediately have a go-to when I introduced this idea above, then you are already struggling trying to think of what you can do to generate more cash. But here is the thing—we live in an age where you can turn practically anything into a means to make money. For most of us, we are not in a position to do things outside of the home, above and beyond our day job, so let's focus on a few ideas that can be done from the comfort of your home.

Babysitting is probably the most obvious and you have built-in entertainment for other people's kids—your own kids. Once a month you could offer a service for "Date Night." Post your offer on Facebook and encourage your circle to take advantage. I promise there are people out there who will take advantage, particularly of your expertise over that of a teenager, which most people use as a go to.

Baking is another great option. I am not a baker and have always spent money on cakes for birthday parties or the occasional cupcakes for various school events. Again, with the power of social media you can start a business page, use your iPhone to snap some shots of your creations, and advertise that you are taking orders for a certain set of dates. I can tell you that personally I opt for these home baker options every single time over the brick and mortar stores for a few reasons. The food is noticeably more fresh, they seem to offer a personal touch, and since they do not have a retail storefront there is no overhead, so generally they are cheaper.

eBay is an option. I use this name only for the concept. There are so many platforms to choose from or to post clothing and other items for resale. This option takes a bit of investment up front, but if you have an eye for scoring good deals, the returns may be worth triple the effort. Consignment stores and Goodwill's are now the capital of another man's treasure. Take time on your lunch break or while the kids are at ball practice and see what you can find to resell. There are many people who do this and are very brand specific in what they seek. Do whatever works for you. The options are endless.

Teaching English to foreign students from your computer. Again, there are all sorts of platforms you can work from to do this. The only requirement is that you must have your bachelor's degree. This is hugely popular among the Asian population, which means the time of day they are available is generally very early morning for us in the States. So much information is available online. Just do a search for teaching English. You will be amazed at what you find.

These are just a few ideas, but there are so many things you can do to earn extra cash. The internet has broadened and expanded the reach of possibility for side hustles.

Working the Plan

Once you have established these baselines, you are ready to lay out your plan. Formulating a purpose for each of these amounts that we have listed. We will start with your **Monthly Residual**. Residual, by definition, is the amount of something you have left after a cycle of use occurs. In this case it is the monthly monies that we have coming in, less the amount of monies we have going out.

As discussed, these are the tried and true, the amounts that as long as you show up in life they are going to occur. Keeping it simple, we understand that the residual amount is what we are currently spending in all the gray areas of life. We are going to change that now and give our residual a renewed purpose and reason for being. Think of monthly residual as your power, your force, the one thing that in this financial game of cards gives you the hand you need to be able to make a change and a positive impact.

Now you will begin to understand why it is was so very important to define all the expenditures you have in a month. Monthly Residual is the amount we are going to start to apply to the list of debts you have created in Step 3, Total Debts Owed. This is where things can get muddy, but I am going to suggest you keep it simple. Start with the smallest amount that is currently owed—this is going to become your **Target**. The Target will always be what you are setting your sights on and throwing your Residual toward until you have fully blasted it away, or less dramatically stated—paid it off.

You are going to breath, sleep, eat, and live with your Target at top of your mind every single day until you have obliterated it.

Now is where we will bring Step 4, Income Generation Opportunity, to the mix. Obviously, the larger your Residual the faster you will be able to eliminate that Target. This will look different for everyone. Some will be more inclined to pick up a hobby and transform it into a business opportunity because they can quickly leverage a talent. Others will be slower and may have to meditate and try many different ideas to see what fits. Give yourself grace with this one. It is not a race and there is no amount of money we are trying to produce. Let it be what it needs to be for you. It is always opportunity, whether you are currently producing an amount of income outside your day job or not. There is opportunity always waiting for you. When circumstances, timing, and effort align, then go with the flow and do not try to force it.

Now we have created Additional Residual, which, you guessed it, will be used as additional income to pay toward that smallest amount of debt. The Income Generation Opportunity will ebb and flow, and will become a part of your regular monthly budgeting practice, as no two months will look the same.

This is all you need to focus on for now. Keep this practice simple and focused until the list in Step 2, Total Debtors Owed, is blank. The financial practice will be extended from there as there are many other steps to take, but, my dear, we must learn to fall gracefully before we can dance with the stars. I can't say it enough —we have to keep it very simple, as a simple practice is much easier to stick to and maintain.

My Personal Thoughts and Reflections on Financial Planning

It is very easy for me to sit here and write these things on the page as if they are nothing and tell you if you follow my simple four steps, you will be home free. However, I have been where you stand, maybe even a farther reach from financial freedom, with limited income and absolutely no light shining at the end of the proverbial tunnel. Money and financial security can be a very helpless emotional ride for a Single Mom, which is the reason for the simplicity in the approach I have outlined for you. Remember to be gentle with yourself as you begin. With that gentleness, however comes an expectation of self-discipline, the act of respecting the goals you have for yourself, and showing up for yourself even when it is hard.

The act of financial planning is not and never will be an act of perfection. It is a pull and tug, a give and take. As a game of intention and strategy, it can become tiresome. But do not fret. All you have to do is show up and bring yourself back to simplicity. Even when you mess up and make that impulse splurge on something you really do not need, forgive yourself quickly, refocus and find your intention once again. That intention will always bring you back home to the bigger plan.

Triggers

You may also find that a lot of people around you are triggered when you tell them you can't go out for drinks or waste time at the mall because you are working on a plan to get yourself out of debt. Please know this is normal. When people hear you are doing something that is a common problem area for most of society, they hear this message from you on a very deep and personal level. People have a tendency to immediately think of themselves and their own situations. They might get a physical lump in their throat and think to themselves, "Oh no, I should be doing this too, and now I am behind." They will rail and push back a bit most likely, trying to sway you from your path. Remember, you always have the choice to follow. And it is not wrong if you choose to spend time with them. Just remember that every financial choice you make that is not supporting the plan is, in effect, slowing the plan down. It doesn't take long for those $5 margaritas to turn into $100 a month that you could have been using to pay off a creditor, effectively putting yourself in a better financial position. Which is more important to you?

Rainy Days

I can't recall the first time I heard the phrase "rainy day fund," but I can remember I was young enough to think it was literally money you spend on rainy days only. I have since come to know only too well what is meant by this play on words. Life happens and sometimes it is expensive. You will have unexpected things come up that require you to spend money you had not planned to spend. I do suggest maintaining some level of emergency fund; how much at this point is really flexible. It is an amount of money you are comfortable setting aside for those rainy days. Even if it is $100, it gives you a pool to pull from that makes it a bit easier to bear when you have things surface that seemingly come out of nowhere.

For my simplistic approach, saving and a true emergency fund will come next, once you get yourself to a place where you can breathe freely and not be constrained by creditors hanging over your head. There is no doubt that things will happen, and you should ensure you have the right insurances in place to cover you when it does. Never ever, no matter the cost, go without carrying health insurance on yourself and your children. This is a hard and fast rule, especially for those of you living in the U.S. Medical care is so expensive and can be financially crippling without the right coverages. Another is car insurance—I fully recommend carrying full coverage on your vehicle unless and until you have enough money in the bank to fully cover the value of your vehicle. If you do not, then you will not be able to replace it in the event something happens. These are a few of the basics you should put in place while you are working the four-step plan.

Finding Support

We are so lucky to live in an age where support for topics of all kinds is literally at your fingertips, and financial planning is absolutely one of these topics. I love to read and listen to podcasts. I believe there is a true connection and reinforcement to be found between strengthening your practice and listening to others speak on the topic. A few of my personal favorites are:

First and foremost—Dave Ramsey. I have listened to Dave since the 90s, and his principles have impacted and changed the trajectory of my financial existence. You will notice many of my ideas and practices around money are rooted in his principles. I worked the envelope system for years and I have maintained a budget monthly since I was barely twenty years old. However, like all things, you tend to find a rhythm and practice that works for you, and I have done just that with the principles I am presenting to you in this chapter.

Next up is Lewis Howes and the School of Greatness. While this is not a financial planning podcast, Lewis is always bringing people on the show who have achieved great things in their lifetimes. I often find that while the conversation might not be centered around money per se, I can translate the ideals of the great achievements of these people into my financial planning practice.

There are also books galore on this topic. choose from. Just find an author who speaks to you. I also recommend if you are going to read a book on financial planning that you opt for the audible version. For me personally it is easier to listen to the topic than read the words on the page. My mind tends to wander when I try to read on this. It may just be me, but it is a tip all the same.

Let it be Simple

Humans have the tendency to over complicate things, to make them hard, or to worry if whatever they are engaging in feels too easy.

When you find yourself in this place when working through your financial planning, remind yourself to let it be easy. The truth is we are only talking and implementing finite math with your plan. We are not worried about interest rates, we are not looking at amortization schedules, and we are not worried about planning for retirement right this second. We are focused on the immediate, the now, the small bites and the big wins that can come when we allow ourselves to embrace the pure simplicity and allow it to be easy.

Closing

In closing this chapter, I want to leave you with this thought. *You* get to decide what your financial future is going to be, what it looks like, and what you are ultimately comfortable with having. If you follow the steps and the method I have provided to you, I can promise you will make an improvement in your situation. Work this plan much like a farmer works the soil and you will reap the harvest in spades.

Tool #7: Be Your Own Best Friend

Chacongas

I was in fifth grade and was taller than anyone else in my class. I had been wearing a bra since the third grade, and by this point I wore a bigger size shoe than any of the women in my family. My hair was thick and unruly, and I had a cowlick in the front that framed my protruding forehead. My nose was also what I felt to be abnormally large. I had this obsession with my nose back in those early days of grade school, with this large lump that sat square in the middle of my face. I would stare at the girls in the lunch room, the older girls—their noses were cute and dainty. You know, perfectly pointed at the end with a cute little lift, as if they had an imaginary string attached to their foreheads that pulled the nostrils at just the perfect angle for nose perfection. Then we had my teeth. Not only were they big and crooked, but they also had weird white spots on them that sometimes were more prominent than others. I remember one day a friend telling me on the way home from the city pool that I had a picture of a rocket ship engraved in my front tooth. She was referencing the shape of the weird white spot that was clearly displayed on the right front tooth.

I felt out of place, out of time, and already, at no more than ten years old, I did not like my body. I didn't understand why every part of me was so big, so large, so in your face larger than life. Or so it seemed to me.

One faithless day in gym class, we were in the locker room changing for whatever physical activities that day held. I heard the laughter from one girl first, then the bellowing amazement from another. I was standing there with my shirt off, completely exposed to the wondering eyes of the girls' locker room. Franticly, I fumbled around in my gym bag searching for my gym shirt. Each time I found myself standing in the middle of that cold dank locker room, I would try desperately to avoid their glances, or even worse, their prying eyes. But this day I would not be so lucky. By the time the third girl had begun to giggle I knew the cat, or big boobs, were out of the bag.

"Chacongas," one of my supposed best friends shouted, "we should call her Chacongas." She strutted around the middle of the locker room with a slight bend in her back holding her hands out in front of her, mocking and pretending she was holding a pair of big breasts. Not only was I awkward on the outside during this phase of life, I was more tangled up on the inside. I just wanted, like any ten-year-old wants, to fit in and be part of the group, the cool kids.

So, they laughed, and I laughed with them. I tried to explain to them, as my grandmother had to me, that I got my large chest from her mom. It ran in the family, it had skipped her and my mom, but it seemed to have taken up with me. My great-grandmother and all her sisters, were the "big women"—that's what my grandma and grandpa would call them. Everyone knew who they were talking about when they would announce that the "big women" were coming to visit. In hindsight, maybe I should have tried to talk to one of the big women about this supposed blessing of big chests, but I never gathered the courage.

That day in the locker room not only did I earn the new nickname of *Chacongas* that would follow me for years to come, but I also became even more self-conscious about the way I looked. I walked away from that gym period with an awareness that other people also noticed my chest, and now I needed to worry about their perceptions as well. Maybe they thought it was funny or maybe they were secretly just jealous that they hadn't made it out of their training bras. I will never know. But I laughed too, and acted like it didn't bother me. I smiled so brightly that no one in that sweaty locker room could possibly see the dark death I felt inside.

This one word, Chacongas, set into motion years of wearing bras that were too small or had the promised minimizing effect and my being completely uncomfortable with the size of my breasts.

In all honesty, I still have times and days that I struggle with certain aspects of myself and my body. There are days I will try on every single article of clothing in my closet in a sweaty rush, trying to find something that makes my muffin top not protrude over the waist line of my jeans. Or I will stare at myself in the mirror and grab and tug on my butt or my thighs and wish they would shrink. This self-defeating behavior is not just reserved for my body. With age and experience, other parts of me have been targeted, like my southern Tennessee accent. It is very prominent. I mean what do you expect from someone who grew up in the South and has lived here her entire forty plus years on the planet. Yet, when I am around people who are not from the same demographic, I can see them lean in when I speak, trying to concentrate on what I am saying so they don't miss it. Which in turn makes me alter my voice and speaking pattern, and often makes me lose track of what I am trying to say altogether. I hear myself speaking, and it gets to a point where I do not recognize the voice that is coming out of my mouth. This begs the question—am I doing this to make it easier for them to hear me, or to make myself try to fit this mold of perfection I try so hard to project?

The point is we are perfectly capable of being our own most harsh critic and the only way to silence that voice is to train it to think differently. The moment you find yourself in a situation where you are falling into a pattern or beating yourself up, bring awareness to it and flip the script in your mind. Even though I have slips from time to time, I have begun to be aware of my tendency to fall into these patterns. I have a larger resistance to allowing my own perception of myself to be measured against a fictitious standard of how I look against a society of any people.

I have come to acknowledge that I am here, in this world and walking on this Earth with my large feet and big boobs for a very specific reason, and any other version of me wouldn't feel the same as I take my steps through. This is a practice of self-acceptance. Be it physical acceptance or a more inward one, the practice and the act are the same.

However, when I found myself on the other side of my marriage and becoming a Single Mom, I felt much on the inside like I did that day in my fifth grade locker room. I felt small and weak, open and vulnerable. For the first time in a long time I wanted to simply shrink into the background of every area of life. The shame was palpable. On the inside I felt like a failure and I was afraid for the world to see it because I didn't know what the world would say.

What would people think of me?

Would they gossip about all potential reasons my marriage had ended?

What did this say about me, as a woman, as wife potential?

What did this say about my worthiness?

Furthermore, what did the title of Single Mom mean to me? I was now a party of one, scared, anxious, and alone. In those early day,s it was as if I was walking alone through all parts of life, alone to school plays or class parties, alone when I dropped the kids off at birthday parties, alone at soccer games, alone at football booster club meeting. My aloneness during this time felt as big as my chest felt when I was in fifth grade. It was like it was part of me, no matter how I tried to minimize it, there it was for all the world to see. I waited anxiously for someone to point their giggles in my direction and call me out on all my aloneness.

The thing is—I lost myself for a moment in a storyline I had conjured up in my own mind.

I wasn't the only Single Parent on Earth. I wasn't the first and I certainly would not be the last. I began to identify these patterns in myself and take active notice of when I felt the urge to shrink and armed myself with the action needed to flip that script in my mind. Some situations were much easier than others. It can be difficult to show compassion to ourselves, but we have no choice. We must learn to reserve compassion for ourselves first and foremost or the lack thereof will limit us.

In this chapter we will focus on practices and areas where you can easily start to make small tweaks and improvements immediately. As you read through these, keep it light and airy and try not to preemptively judge what will work for you and what will not. It is important anytime we dip our toes into something new that we keep an open mind to the process, even when it feels out of step for you. So, let's dive in and explore how can we love ourselves, give ourselves kindness, and effectively become our own best friends.

The Inner Critic

I am sure you have heard referenced the angel and devil sitting on opposing shoulders when trying to balance a decision. The idea being that there are two opposite views representing each side of our brain, where the right things and the wrong things live.

The angel will whisper to you to be loving, considerate of others, and to always keep the right thing at front of mind, while the devil will mutter to you that hatred and anger are the best choices, to forget what the others need, and to forget about the right thing, do the thing that benefits you.

Well I would like to introduce a third, often more prominent figure to the imaginary gossip party. We will call her The Inner Critic. She sits on her pedestal high above the center of your head and can be counted on to beat down the angel and devil so hard that even they are afraid to speak and risk feeling her wrath.

At times she will whisper. Her tone is soft and blunt, tainted with the sounds of second guessing yourself. She can be heard playing on repeat in your head, over and over as she grumbles:

"How could you say that?"

"You should have said this!"

"Why did you do that?"

"What if you would have done that instead?"

"They really must think you are so stupid!"

"How could you ever think such a thing?"

"Why did you wear that dress? You look so huge and you have a fat roll showing."

"Why can't I look like her?"

"Am I the only person in the world who doesn't know what that word means?"

"How could I possibly be so stupid?"

I know you have been there, standing in the dark shadow of your own mind, listening to the hate that only your very own Inner Critic can spew. Once you hear the contempt this beast breathes into your mind, it cannot be unheard. Some days are better than others, there are times that you can shut her down or counterbalance her wrath. On those days it is easier to breathe through the shit she spews and find that place deep inside of your own heart where your truth lives and you hold your value tight…a sacred place where only you hold the key to access.

So how do we fight against this beast that is seemingly bigger than we are? She is such a bully…how do we shut her down? The first step is acceptance—simple acceptance in understanding this is normal. No one can be harder on us than we can be on ourselves and it is a natural tendency to criticize and berate ourselves. It is quite simply a part of our nature and to some extent it is not entirely a bad thing. If we didn't have some degree of awareness we would be slower to make improvements and changes in our lives. Those little tweaks are for the things that no longer serve us or help us grow. However, there is an intangible line we so often cross that we need to really focus on and learn how to manage. Once we have accepted that we are perfectly normal for feeling this way and give ourselves the grace, we are all set to move to the next steps.

Write down the thoughts you are having and read them aloud to yourself. The preference is to catch it right when they are happening and do it so in the moment, you have yourself hear how inaccurate and irrational these thoughts can be.

Once you have read the list all the way through, write a counterpoint for each thought. For example, "How could I possibly be so stupid?" would be met with a counter statement of, "I am very intelligent and have accomplished many things because of my brain." Writing this truth and the reinforcement of speaking it into existence breaks the pattern or the loop that is created by the voice of the Inner Critic.

This is the most effective practice to bring us back to level-minded thinking and prevent us from jumping down the rabbit hole of patterns that allow us to beat ourselves up. When this happens, if you are not in a place where it is practical to stop and write/read aloud, then take out your phone if possible and make a note of the thoughts you are having so you can revisit this practice when you can find solitude.

You also have the option of meditation. Take sixty seconds to close your eyes and mentally play out the above without the writing and speaking aspect. The main goal is to acknowledge then counterbalance right away. You can do this by whatever means best suits your style and resonates for you.

Another tip is reflection. This is a powerful tool in so many areas of our lives. It is simple, yet very effective, in aiding us in the practice of identifying the symptoms of many of the issues that arise for us. Journaling is an effective way of reflecting. You may prefer it to visuals or walking it out in your mind. Whatever works for you.

A few things to focus on and be sure to bring to the surface are: What was the environment you were in when the Inner Critic spoke up? Who are the people you were around? Were you in a place you love or a space where you feel safe? Were you nervous when you heard her voice? All of these will help you begin to paint a picture of understanding that will provide you with a road map of the sorts of triggers for your Inner Critic, which in turn will help you better prepare for her in the future.

In building a defense against the damage the Inner Critic can cause, we essentially retrain our brains to deal with her bothersome voice in a much healthier manner. This practice is much like anything else. The more you do it, the more effective you will find it to be. It takes consistent effort and like many other things in this book, effort in that you must be very honest with yourself. No one else can step in and help you on this one. You are the only one living inside your own head, so be diligent in your practice.

Drop the Negativity

There is something to be said, a lot of something to be said, for mindset and perception. We all know that one person who drains the joy out of all situations just by refusing to see or accept any sort of positive outlook or outcome. This is one area where I have had to try hard myself to course correct.

I have never really had the tendency to be a full-on pessimist, so if you are reading this and thinking this doesn't apply to you, stay with me here. Even the tiniest bit of negativity can have a huge ripple effect within your nervous system. Your heart, your lungs, your brain, and your spine are much like a central highway for all the parts and pieces that are uniquely you. When you allow a negative thought into that system, which begins in your brain, it will race down the internal highway, wreaking full-blown havoc along its path.

Since the thoughts and mindsets that are laced with the negativity originate in your brain, this is where we will focus our efforts to rectify and send them down a different path. The first step is in the recognition of the thought or the feeling that begins to grow inside us. We must first teach ourselves to recognize when we feel it coming on.

Let's look at an example. Your ex-husband is scheduled to take the kids to the zoo. The kiddos are super pumped about this outing. He will pick them up Saturday morning, picnics packed and sunscreen in tote, ready for a day of safe exploring of the wildlife. You are a bit envious, but over all you are happy. The joy on your kids' faces as they talk about going to the zoo with their dad fills your heart with love. Then Saturday arrives and when your ex shows up at the door with his head hung and shoulders slumped, you immediately know the zoo trip you have played out for a week with your kids isn't happening. You will get to be the one who aids in dropping the bomb on their tiny little hearts then turning to build up how fun something else will be instead.

Of course you will feel all the emotions—frustration, anger, disappointment, etc. This is where you need to step in with a rational approach and realize you have a choice here in how you are going to engage this situation. You could absolutely go down the path of negativity; it is certainly warranted. Every single emotion you are feeling, laced with the negativity, is valid. However, it is important to ask yourself this question: Is that negativity going to serve you and the people involved in this situation to produce an ideal result? The answer clearly is no, it will not. Even more importantly, it will impact the people, in this case your kids, in a more detrimental way when they see your negativity come to the surface.

An ideal response to this example is acceptance, flow, and release. The outcome is sealed, you can't control or change it, so the ideal response is to *accept* that it is what it is. The way this goes down is not within the realm of your control, so *flow* in the situation. Do not try to hold on so tight to how badly it sucks that the zoo isn't happening and controlling the disappointment of the kids, but instead *release*. Release the need to drive an end result in any fashion and let it flow. This type of response will help everyone around you by visibly providing an example and giving an energy to the situation that will provide grounding and peace.

As critical as it is to work on ourselves, we also have to be diligent in protecting ourselves from the negativity of others. One way to think of this is you do not have to make a choice to cut these negative people out of your life necessarily, but rather make a conscious effort to spend more time around those people who lift us up as opposed to bringing us down. This act of natural selection will evolve organically as we continue to choose to be around those positive people to whom we are naturally more attracted. Positivity is like a drug—once you find a kindred spirit who lifts your soul when you are in close proximity to them, you will want more and more of that in your life. Set boundaries within your space, especially as it pertains to your mental state and health. Do not be afraid to shut out the negativity of other people. That is one thing you can control.

One is not a lonely number

It was a bright and sunny day; the birds were chirping and flowers blooming. A new Spring was making her grand entrance this particular Saturday in April, and with Spring came the kick off of my daughter's soccer season. It was still a bit chilly but that didn't matter. We drove to the soccer field with the moonroof open and the music blasting. She was pumped and ready to go and I was following suit. Coffee in one hand and chair in the other, we raced toward the field in the direction of the right color of uniforms we could see in the distance.

As we got closer, we could see faces start to emerge from the figures, confirming we were indeed heading in the right direction. About this time, Kyleigh lets out a squeal. "Dad!" she shouted, and turned her little body in his direction. I slowed down, but was still heading my feet in that general direction until I saw another figure, a female figure, step up beside him. Then my feet were not quite sure what to do, to walk toward, to walk to another spot, or to simply run the other direction.

You see, even despite everything up to this point, my ex and I had continued to sit together at the kids' events. We were not mad at each other over the divorce and there did not seem to be animosity between us at all. As a matter of fact, I was proud of how much like adults we were handling the new arrangement. Look at us, being the best parents to our kids, despite the fact we could no longer stand to be together. Finally, we were getting something right.

But once another female stepped onto the scene, I was thrown very quickly out of the spotlight reel. This was no longer a story about a couple of divorced parents trying to figure things out and make the best of a non-ideal situation for their kids. The plot was growing and the cast expanding, and I was unsure of how I fit.

So, I took my seat and found refuge many chairs away from my ex and his female companion, and sat anxiously awaiting the end of the game. But I learned that day—the end of the game is probably worse than arriving at the game because you do not want to force your kids into a strange situation.

The game is over, and excitement is thick in the air. The sweaty little soccer players turn to head toward the sideline filled with cheering parents. Mom is on the far left and Dad is on the far right. Which way is your kid supposed to go?

The moment of relief I felt when the game ended was quickly replaced with a huge dilemma more of, "Which way should my feet go? Stand still or move in the direction of ex and female companion?"

I went to so many games, football for my son and soccer for my daughter, where I was alone and inevitably after every single one, I would move slowly in the direction of my ex and his female companion. We exchanged a few awkward pleasantries then stared across the field waiting for the kids to come running our direction. In the early days, each time this happened, I could feel myself wanting to shrink and feel small. But every single time I would stand alone in that awkwardness and endure until I could finally reach the solitude of my own vehicle, sometimes with a kid in tow, other times alone.

There are fewer things in this world that will make you feel more alone than when you see or hear your ex has found another. I have found this to be especially true if you are still single yourself. It is as if the world has set a magnifying glass on top of your head and asked, "So, where is your plus one?" For me, it wasn't even that I cared he was with someone. It wasn't about him at all. It was about me.

It was about how it made me feel insecure about another woman being involved in our children's lives. What if she did this mothering thing better than me or what if they liked her better? What things would my kids experience in this new and exciting hodge-podge family environment that I would never get to be a part of?

The list of insecurities would continue to rise to the surface, forming as a lump in my throat until I could forcibly swallow them down and check myself. This situation, even though you might feel it deeper and stronger, is no different than any other that comes up in our lives. We just have to be intentional in the face of the panic and "what ifs" to take a very close look at what we are thinking and why. It is so easy to slip down a slope of despair and hopelessness when we feel that we are standing alone.

Chin up, sister. You might be standing by yourself, but you are not walking alone in this world. Wherever you choose to put your feet, you are leaving an imprint on the world that sees you, and your kids see you, brave and bold. Each time you refuse to shrink and stand in your situation no matter how uncomfortable, you use that strength that is inside and you begin to gain trust in yourself. Your very own ability to endure, to stand tall, and to refuse to shrink. There is no one on Earth who can have your back like you can have it for yourself.

    You are your own best friend.

Tool #8:
Stigmas

Soccer Moms

The first months after becoming a single mom felt much like trying to learn how to ride a bike or roller skate for the first time. You lean too much to the right then quickly shift your weight to center but inevitably end up falling on your ass because you overshot to the left. Your elbows are scraped and your bum is sore, but nothing is more bruised than your ego. At least this was the case for me.

I completely get it—there are so many women who plan this journey, they want to have children and haven't found the right partner yet. They plot and plan and head out into the journey of bringing kids into this world all on their very own accord. I respect those women so much and even though I do not know any of them personally, I can imagine they are the types that have all their I's dotted and T's crossed. They know what they want and they set out to get it, pivoting and maneuvering along the way.

I was not one of these women.

I spent so much of the early years of motherhood trying to copy what the other moms did. I would take the kids to the park to play and watch incessantly at how the other moms would put their kids carefully in the swings or place them safely on top of the slide, holding on to them until they were half way down, ensuring their protection.

I would immediately measure their grace and nurturing playground spirit against mine, which was more of a, "go figure it out kid" kind of approach. I would end up guilting myself away from the bench where I preferred to be, waiting and watching, and I would insert myself into their playtime like a playground guardian so that I measured up to the other mothers around me.

The truth is I knew nothing about being a mother, and being a nurturer is not an attribute that comes to me naturally. When my son was born, I did not even know how to change a diaper; his dad had to teach me. I remember when we came home from the hospital, our home was full of family and friends who had brought food to welcome us, all offering their love and support. It should have been a time of overwhelming joy, but all I could feel was the shock that the hospital let me leave with another human in my care.

I sat myself square in the middle of my son's nursery and cried. I was scared to death and had absolutely no idea what I was doing with myself, let alone what I would do with a baby. I felt my way through those early years. I tried on all kinds of mommy type characteristics, keeping what suited me and shedding those that did not.

It wasn't until my son began to play soccer that I was introduced to Soccer Moms. Sure, I had heard this title before and understood that Soccer Moms were the ones behind the wheel of the minivan, carting dozens of kids to and from practices and games. Juice boxes and snack size cookies packages in tow, she was the champion among the Mom ranks. She could plan the car pool pickups, manage the after-practice snack menu, delegate the before and after game clean ups, and organize booster support like nobody's business.

From my purview, these women always seemed to have flawless skin, perfect hair, and be the most popular in a group of women who would follow in their footsteps, desperate to be the second or third in command. Who wouldn't want to be a Soccer Mom?

The first few years that my son played, I gladly stepped into the role. At some point we even traded our SUV for a dark green minivan. I was so far into it I had a special box of snacks in the back of my van that I kept just in case those moms with the habitual tired faces who hadn't figured out how to juggle it all forgot it was their turn to bring after practice snacks for the players.

I looked forward to the practices, which took place no less than two days a week. That was my social hour and the time I really could mix with others. I made friends with all the Moms, talking about how little Johnny seemed to be really loving the game and how he might go on to play in the pros. Or how little Suzi really seemed to be coming out of her shell; she was so quiet when the season started.

I was a Soccer Mom Sensation in my own mind.

By the time I became a Single Mom, I had two kids actively playing sports. Both played soccer and my son also played football. We had sports going around the clock, year-round. I was in for a reality check as it pertained to my time and priorities.

I was now the single head of household, and things that used to be easily divided were now my sole responsibility. Grocery shopping, house cleaning, laundry, mowing the lawn, landscaping, taking trash off, cooking, bath time, homework, etc. While these things had always been on the radar, previously I had help. Going to practice two days a week quickly began to feel like more of another thing I had to do than something I wanted to do.

I withdrew from the Soccer Mom social scene and soon found myself taking advantage of the time the kids were at practice by going to the grocery store or running errands, or simply taking a walk alone through the park. I developed a keen awareness to the value of my time and how limited it was, and as a result the things that got my attention started to shift and change.

For all the time I had spent silently judging those moms who seemed too tired to remember snacks or volunteer for clean-up, I now had to face the reality that I was becoming one of them. The fact is I was ignorant to what was really painted on the faces of these women. Sure they were tired, but they were also stretched thin. Pulled and probed in many directions simultaneously, trying to keep their own kids alive, seldom a minute to think about anything other than their to-do list, let alone a freaking juice box for someone else's kids. They were happy and content with being able to remember to feed their own kids and have them show up at practice. Finally, I understood, and the reality of that clearly as it smacked me square in the face.

The karma that was created by my passive aggressive judgement of other women choosing not to participate in the Soccer Mom Reality was chased down by a huge dose of humility, understanding, and self-realization.

I would no longer find the mom I wanted to be on the playgrounds or on the practice soccer fields. If I continued to look outside of myself, I would only be measured against women who I no longer had the time or desire to be. Truth be told, I never wanted to be them to begin with. I was just too insecure and scared to be who I was at my core, always looking outward, waiting for the world to tell me who to be.

Following this shift in my life, I began to take a closer look at the women around me, the ones who continued to exist in the Soccer Mom Reality, examining not only what they did but also trying to discern why they did it. I would watch closely their faces hurrying in and out, on and off, scooting kids along. Tying shoe laces, lagging gym bags overstuffed with extra clothing and equipment, water bottles pressed to their chests because they lacked a free hand, their purses slung partially over one shoulder, a book sticking clumsily out of the open zipper IF they were lucky enough to remember to bring something for themselves.

I had to ask myself, Why?

Why do we do it?

Do we really want to, or do we feel that we are supposed to?

Soccer is just an example. There are so many areas of our lives that could be plugged in here. Please do not misunderstand me. The point is not exclusively about soccer. The point is when do we as women, as mothers, decide that it is okay to shelve the titles and just be?

When did simply showing up to watch your kid play in the game become uncool?

And why do we not bring that level of ease back to motherhood?

Our kids could care less about the damn juice boxes. They would be just as happy to drink from the garden hose or share a bottle of water with the kids on the team. We are putting the pressure on ourselves, and in some cases raising the bar and expectation for those other moms (single or not) without realizing it.

Let's create a simpler existence where we support each other as moms, as women, to be something bigger and better for the greater good of our femininity.

Let's challenge each other to make "Soccer Mom" a secondary identity as we help each other build upon our unique existence, something that will make our children proud.

Let's admit that even though we have families who need our support in our role as Mom, we are not the glue that holds everything together, and this facade of perfectness that we work tirelessly to create means nothing if we are left empty inside.

Let's take care to be women first, the not-so-perfect, mess of hormones, chocolate loving, wine drinking, sometimes horny sometimes not, women who seek out satisfaction for ourselves in things we desire that will ultimately make us better mothers, wives, sisters, daughters, and even Soccer Moms.

Societal Stigmas

For the most part, I have always been a creature that thrives on structure. The laundry gets done on Saturday mornings, lawn is mowed on Saturday afternoons, dishwasher is run on Thursday evening and unloaded Friday morning so it is empty for the weekend, and the grocery shopping is done on Sunday. Truth be told, I had to implement this type of structure to be able to avoid letting anything slip when I became a Single Mom.

I have never been a fan of going to the grocery store anyways, but I especially hated when I forgot something during the weekend run and had to go during the week after a long day at work. But it happened from time to time and it never seemed to fail that I would forget an ingredient for something I promised the kids I would make. So, I had that added guilt of going to the store to get it rather than adjusting the menu for the week.

This was the case when I found myself in the grocery store line on a rainy Tuesday afternoon. I was only two days into the work week, and it felt like a month of bullshit had had already happened. Let's just say it wasn't my week. And here I stood, waiting in line with wet feet (open toe heels do not pair well with rainy days) waiting for my turn to check out.

I noticed the person in front of me right away. She had her back to me with a baby, probably one year old, slung over her shoulder. The baby's cute little checks and slobbery mouth turned into a smile when he/she spotted me and my heart melted. Isn't it funny how the world can simply melt away when we see a cute baby or a puppy or a baby chick? It is like the sweetness of candy for adults, such a treat to see, especially when we aren't the ones caring for it.

We continued to progress through the line until it was the lady and the baby's turn to check out. She placed the baby in the carrier that set atop the buggy and turned to face the cashier. This is when I noticed the lady was a young mother, likely no older than twenty-five. She had WIC coupons in one hand and the other hand was placed calmly on her midsection, where underneath a protruding belly held another baby.

The baby was not happy with being placed in the carrier and started to cry, which I could tell was agitating this young girl and the cashier. The woman behind the register was an older lady with a stern face. As I examined her face, I was hoping to spot a bit of compassion or a hint of empathy, but instead, I watched her eyes as she pushed her glasses back up onto her nose. She looked at the coupon in the girl's hand, the groceries on the conveyer belt, the baby in the buggy and the baby in the belly, then straight to the girl's face. She would not be serving any compassion today. I knew it before she spoke.

"You need to organize your WIC items before you present your coupon," she said to the girl. It was then that I noticed there was no ring on this young girl's finger. She was in this grocery store alone, selecting her WIC items alone, walking through life alone.

She reached back toward the groceries, keeping one hand placed on the baby in an attempt to soothe and calm and quiet the crying. The cashier became more frustrated at the girl's attempt to do what she was asking than she was before and was not offering any assistance.

I stepped from around the buggy and said, "I can help, let me see your coupons." Her eyes met mine and without a word, she handed me the coupons. I pulled out the eggs, cheese, and cereal and forcefully set them at the front of the line for the cashier. I met her dead in the eyes and said, "This should do it," then jabbed the coupon in her direction. She muttered "Thank you," darting her eyes back to the young girl, scolding her without a word, and proceeded to complete the transaction.

Lucky for me I only had a few items. The one thing I had forgotten to get during the previous weekend's grocery run and other things I threw in the buggy on a whim. When I stepped up to meet the cashier, she breathed heavy and said, "Women these days, going and getting themselves pregnant when they are still kids themselves. No daddy in the picture, raising these kids on their own and depending on the government to help them." I focused my attention on the credit card pad and clenched my jaw tight. I was raised to respect my elders and didn't want to make a complete ass of myself, so I simply responded with, "I guess we never know what other people are going through, do we?" I left it at that in hopes that my comment would stick and possibly make a difference in the next girl that passed through her line. We all know it likely did not.

This is an example of one stigma we Single Moms face, one ugly side of the coin. The stigma that we are irresponsible women who are incapable of taking care of ourselves so we have children out of wedlock so we can qualify for government assistance. But the Single Mom Stigma Coin has two sides, the other for those who *do* work and provide for their kids; they are stigmatized for being irresponsible and are commonly shamed for missing out or not being involved enough with their kids. It depends on the voice of public opinion you tap into. Much like politics, everyone has an opinion that is rarely informed by experience, but rather what someone else tells them to think.

I want to make it clear that I understand there are folks out there who game the system. They do so with intention and clarity. Not only Single Moms, but for other outlets as well—disability, workers compensation, etc. I am not naïve, and I understand this happens, but I refuse to accept this is the standard.

Do we really believe this type of intention is the norm? Do we insist on telling ourselves these people put all their energy into plotting and planning how to be taken care of instead of simply finding themselves in a bad situation? While we can all accept that this does happen, do we really allow our compassion for others to dissipate because we want to believe stigma applies to everyone who crosses our path?

I have encountered so many of these cookie cutter type stigmas during my time as a Single Mom. You will notice those who carry their opinions like a badge of honor also follow it with a question that validates their views.

Single Moms are sexually promiscuous. How else would they end up in such a situation?

Single Moms have too much baggage. How could they not?

Single Moms can't be depended on in their jobs. How can they be both diligent and sole caretaker of kids?

Single Moms made their bed, now they can lie in it. How did she not know she was making a mistake?

Here is what I know for certain: opinions are like assholes and everyone has one. My grandmother told me this when I was young; she probably said "butt" in all fairness, nonetheless the point remains. I would add to that—not only do they have opinions but they are mostly insolent and uninformed. They draw from societal stigmas, jumping on the bandwagon of group think to help form their beliefs.

If we allow ourselves to spend our time wondering why this is the way of our culture, then we lose precious time to focus on ourselves and our families. Stereotyping people has been a way of humans since the beginning of time. Truth be told, we all have a tendency become prey to it if we are not intentional about avoiding it. Race, gender, sexual preference, ethnicity, athletes, the list of groups that fall into the broader stigmas in our culture is vast and long. In this section, we will not concern ourselves with the psychology of this phenomenon, but rather how to debunk it and flip the bandwagon upside down.

Let people know when they are stigmatizing

I had the perfect opportunity in the grocery store with the overly judgmental clerk to correct her, and I completely missed out on it because my emotions took over. But the point is, it doesn't always have to be *you* who is standing up for yourself. We, the collective, this society of Single Mothers, can help educate the general population, our family, and our closest friends that these old ways of thinking about women need to be discarded. One of the ways we change the way people think, interestingly enough, is to tell them what, why, and how to think about people.

It took time for me to come around to thinking of my title of Single Mom as more of a badge of honor and less of a curse, but I noticed that when I started to speak of it in a positive light, I received a more positive reaction from those around me. Choose to be part of rewriting the narrative around these stigmas every single opportunity you get. And remember, we live in a digital world where you can spread your voice over so many outlets. Take to the web, social media, blogs, vlogs, write an article, or volunteer your time to speak out in a forum like a podcast.

Speak out loudly and often. Your words will translate into a new truth.

Empowerment over Shame

When we make a decision to be at peace with where we are in our life story and embrace the situation, we begin to exude a sense of power that allows us to stand in the thick of the deep waves of shame, as they will inevitably come at us. This shame that is heavy and fraught with the unknowing, the undoing, and the unforgiving, will weigh us down if we shrink and allow it to place itself on top of us. The simplest way to avoid this is to rise and stand in our truth, which is that which we choose to tell ourselves.

We need to set hard boundaries by making an agreement with ourselves. It's almost like an emotional barrier that will act as a stronghold against any ideas the general public may hold about us when we refuse to see ourselves in the same light that others may try to shine on us. The truth is, what people think of you has more to do with them and their own issues than it has to do with you. Also, what others think of you is none of your business. Focus on what you think of you, that is all that matters. As Dr. Seuss taught us, "Those who matter don't mind, and those who mind don't matter."

Get support

Support can look like various things. I had a best friend who was also a Single Mom. We met each other just months after she had gotten a divorce and I was less than a year away from mine. We both had two kids, close to the same ages, and we worked together. Her friendship was like a Godsend to me. There are also groups that form that are free to join. Get online and look into Meetup.com or Facebook Groups for those in person options that already exist in your area. If you do not find something, then start one yourself. One of the best ways you can prop yourself up is by understanding you are not alone. The sheer knowing that there are other people experiencing similar circumstances and can relate to what you are going through can do wonders to improve your day to day outlook on life.

Go see a therapist. Here we go, yet another commonly stigmatized topic. You may even find yourself thinking, "I do not need therapy." Truth is, therapy is one of the best ways to open yourself completely and receive unbiased support and guidance. Trained professionals often can identify root causes of some of our most problematic behaviors and provide us with the tools we need to correct, heal, or simply change the issue. Therapy is action-oriented, and when we take action to redirect something, we automatically create hope which infuses us with the reassurance we can manage through the storms.

This too shall pass

All circumstances are temporary, and while we may forget this while we walk in them, we will come out the other side one way or another. We are not our situations, nor are we defined by the state of affairs in our lives. Our lives are much like a book—we crack it open to peek inside, we will see a plethora of words strung into stories that navigate us through from a beginning to an end. What is often under-credited is the massive mushy middle; this is where the brunt of the development happens. The middle is where we learn who the characters are and find ourselves latching on to them, relating and empathizing through their journeys. The middle is where the learning is abundant, the bumps are punishing, and the victories are gratifying. Sometimes when I am in the thick of a plotline, I find myself wanting to skip to the end. I just can't bear not knowing how the story will end, knowing that if I did this the end just wouldn't be as sweet, as gratifying. The middle is part of the story, and is just as important to the overall thread of the tale as the beginning or the end.

You are in the middle right now, the tricky, sticky, sometimes icky middle. One day you will look back and reflect on how these days challenged and changed you. Your kids will be formed by them, too. They and you will learn to appreciate these days, so embrace them now. Everything you are going through is a part of your story and the legacy you will leave behind. Some days will be hard; you will find yourself hiding in the closet crying, swearing you can't take another day. Others will be filled with love and laughter and you will find yourself thankful for every moment. Life is fleeting, every single moment. This is part of your journey. Enjoy it while it lasts, as this part, too, shall pass.

Tool #9: Rewrite Your Happily Ever After

Peaches, Pennies, and Princesses

The first memory I have of weddings was from when I was seven years old. My aunt, who was only thirteen when I was born, was getting married and this was to be a grand event. For over a year, every family gathering would evolve into a discussion about some topic around this wedding. How many layers would the cake be? What type of icing would be used? How many bridesmaids? How many groomsmen? Who would be included on the guest list and who would not? Would the gazebo be done by then?

    All these things in my child brain just did not equate. To this point in my young life, I was only vaguely familiar with the concept of weddings and marriage from the Little Golden Books that my aunt bought me. She always made sure I had all the books that are notorious for feeding little girl dreams of glass slippers, white horses, and handsome princes. I never saw a mention of the details she was throwing around in these stories. I didn't even know what a gazebo was or why it was needed for the wedding.

As the day grew closer, all the details started to solidify. The bride's color of choice was peach—not just peach, y'all, but its 1982 version of Southern belle, Atlanta wanna-be peach. I can still remember looking at myself in the mirror once I was able to maneuver into my dress. The lace trimmings and sheer overlays of fabric made getting into the arm holes more like trying to find your way out of a labyrinth. So many materials, so much dress, and even more southern peach color.

My peach ensemble was topped off with an umbrella that, believe or not, was even more gaudy than the dress. As I stared at the reflection in the floor length mirror with the hustle and bustle of women getting ready for the big moment, the ideas of a wedding, of marriage, slowly entrenched themselves in my brain.

This is what it is all about, I thought as my gaze left my own reflection and found my aunt just a few feet behind me. She looked like Cinderella with her girlfriends swooning around her, one tucking and pinching the dress in all the right places, another circling her with a comb and bottle of hairspray, smoothing down all the stray hairs around her fresh wife-to-be face. The only things missing were the Fairy Godmother, the mice, and the sound of "bippity boppity boo" echoing through the room.

We had practiced the line up the night before during rehearsal. My part was simple. On my right side, I would be ushered down the aisle by a squeaky voice preteen. On my left side I was to carry my umbrella, making my wrist limp so it would tilt at just the perfect angle to jet to the side and not hit my preteen escort in the head.

We were to proceed to the frontmost row of chairs where we would go our separate ways. He to the right and me to the left. I would go then on my own, to find my place behind the lady that did the very same song and dance right before me. But I had to be extra careful to stand in just the right spot which was marked with a bright shiny new copper penny. There were so many things for a seven-year-old to remember. I distinctly remember looking down at that penny for the entire ceremony. I wanted to bend over and pick it up but knew that would be a terrible idea, so I resisted.

I do not remember walking back down the aisle when it was all over. I doubt many people cared how I held my umbrella at that point, and I didn't have any coins that I was on a secret treasure hunt for. All I do remember is when my aunt's Volkswagen Bug pulled out of the driveway at the end of the night, the cans clunking loudly behind it and her friends running behind the car to see it off, I thought to myself, *I want to do this someday.*

I Love You Forever

Some years later I got my shot at the princess wedding, albeit not the financial fiasco my aunt's had been. I paid for the majority of my wedding so there were no swan ice sculptures randomly placed on snack tables to create a romantic ambiance. We had the basics: a wedding dress I bought on clearance at a local prom dress store, décor for the reception me and my friends made from hand, and a wedding cake—a notable three layers my mom made for us. The church bells rang, and the pews were full of family and friends as we walked through the act of becoming husband and wife.

Looking back, it is so abundantly clear to me now that neither of us fully understood just what we were signing up for. "I love you forever" was the signature of choice my friends and I all used for our letters to boyfriends in high school in my day.

You see, it was the 90s and we young ladies were fueled by the love ballads playing on MTV that promised us, *"I'll never let you go"* and *"I'll love you forever and a day."* We were hormonal bodies of flesh, walking around with Aqua Net in our veins and desperation for that deep love we sang about in our hearts.

We would spend more time in class writing these letters to our boyfriends than we ever spent listening to the teachers. And of course we would sign every single one with the standard, "Love you forever," add our name, bend the paper in a cute fold, then drop it in his locker and call it a day, secretly looking around for our next target of affection.

Clearly this situation was not high school. Here I found myself standing in front of this guy who would become my kids' father, telling him in front of all the people in the pews, the preacher, and God, that I would be bound to love him forever. In sickness, in health, in all of the quantifiable ways that people have vowed to love each other for all eternity.

I promised this sacred promise, literally to God and everyone, knowing full well as I stood there in my discounted dress and with my sweaty palms that I didn't believe a word I was saying. The words felt so distant and empty on my tongue, much like a signature on a letter that talks about less pressing matters such as sneaking off to make out under the bleachers during a pep rally or how big of assholes are parents are being and trying to understand how they could possibly ground us from the school dance.

But this was no letter that would land in a locker. This was a promise, a contract, a binding commitment. So, I swallowed down the truth and smiled through my doubt. The stage was set and there would be no exit left.

I repeated after the preacher and vowed with my obligatory, "I will love you forever."

Guess what? I lied.

My fairytale ending would not be met with a silver or gold plated recognition. Hell, we narrowly made it through ten years.

It wasn't all him and it wasn't all me. We just didn't fit and I am pretty sure we both knew it very early on. The older we grew, the harder it was to ignore the truth. We were like the analogy of a round peg and a square hole—we were not made to go together without some obnoxious maneuvering that made me tired and him resentful.

The truth was I felt a bit of relief when it all came to a screaming halt. It was if the jig was up, the cat was out of the bag, and even though I was so sad for my kids and fearful of what that meant for our futures, I felt a sense of relief for no longer having to participate in the charade. Of course, I had all the fears that all women who have stood in this position have: financial concerns, what will friends and families think, telling the kids, deciding who gets what, and, of course, asking ourselves if this was it, our one shot at the happily ever after we had been promised since childhood. What if we ended up alone?

When my mom and dad divorced, I remember distinctly her saying to me one day in the car, "I will never get married again." She was so sure in that statement and I, not knowing any differently, took her statement very literally.

So, when she announced to me many years later that her and my now stepdad had gone to the courthouse to get married, I was furious. All I could think and say to her was, "but you said..." I couldn't possibly understand at that point in my life and wouldn't for many many years to come.

I made a similar statement when I found myself a divorcèe; actually, mine was more like, "There is no way in hell I will ever, ever, no matter what, get married again." I wasn't a female scorned; I am the one who was the final decider of the marriage ending. He wanted to try to salvage the relationship, to hang on and "stick it out for the kids," he said.

But really, we knew it was over, and once I decided we were going down that path to end it, there was no turning back. Nonetheless, I could not imagine putting myself in that position ever again.

I had resigned myself to the fact my Prince Charming got lost in Never Never Land, or maybe he fell off his pristine white horse, broke his neck, and died. I didn't know, I didn't care, I was done. Period.

But secretly, in my heart of hearts, I knew I did not want to walk through life alone. I wanted to have a partner, a confidant, so I knew I would open myself to a relationship and those possibilities. But I never intended to make it legal, ever again.

But as we all know, things change.

Dating, Hooking Up, and Hanging Out

The first time I had a boyfriend I was somewhere around ten years old. I recall announcing to my Grandma during my customary Saturday night sleepovers that, "I was going with Andy."

All I remember about her response was a question, "Where exactly are you going?"

I was confused by her confusion. Her face was completely perplexed, which drove even more dismay through my brain.

How did she not know what I meant? Going Together was huge in my world. This was what we called it, or at least what all the kids at school called it. Tammy was going with Paul, LeeAnn was going with Richard, Jennifer was going with Matt, everyone was going with someone and I wanted to be going too. And finally, it had happened, and here I was left to ponder exactly where I was going, why I was going there, and maybe heading in that direction with Andy wasn't as special as I thought.

I have always found the slang and cultural actions associated with dating to be pretty obnoxious. We have gone from Going Steady in the 70s, to Friends With Benefits in the 90s, to Swiping Left or Right in present day. I feel like we over complicate one of our most basic human needs for connection by putting all these parameters and categorizations around them.

Dating after divorce just adds a whole additional layer of complexity to the mix. And if that complexity isn't enough, those stigmas we talked about in the last chapter follow us to dating as Divorced Women and Single Moms.

They have a bit of a different flavor, but the connotation is the same—all the unchanged bandwagon, cookie cutter bullshit that society uses to slice and dice us into categorical boxes because they don't know what else to do with us.

I mean, we must have baggage, right? We must not be cut out for marriage or the marrying type, right? We must be gold-diggers and expect to have someone else pay everything for us, right? We must be tainted, failures of sorts, because we couldn't make it work, right? We are desperately seeking daddies for our children, right?

Most disappointingly of all is that all these stereotype assumptions are emphatically *not* rooted in truth. More often than not, they happen to be the exact opposite of the expectation of us as Single Mothers.

Let me say this—not every person you may be interested in dating is going to subscribe to these outdated ways of thinking. And if they do, he or she is likely not progressive enough in their own lives to be in yours anyway. If you have made it to this point in this book, you, my dear soul, are by definition an enlightened woman with a belief that rules, and stigmas are for people who live life led by fear and are unable to challenge the status quo, or, even worse, form opinions of their own. Anything less in a partner is selling yourself short.

The most memorable date I had during my journey as a Single Mom was tainted with stigma before we pulled out of the driveway. It was such a let-down, too. It completely threw me off my game because I had not been so excited about a date in such a very long time.

The story was a boy meets girl, completely unplanned and unexpected. It was a Thursday evening and me and several of my friends had planned a girls' night out. We had dinner and a few drinks, the chit chat was flowing smoothly, and everyone was laughing and having such a good time we didn't want to call it a night. The group decided to taxi to a nearby bar and keep the conversation and the wine flowing.

I didn't notice him when we walked in, and I truly have no idea when he noticed me, but when our eyes locked it was instant attraction. Like something you see in a movie starring Julia Roberts—camera focuses on her face when she spots the handsome stranger across the room. The lust on the screen is palpable.

The moment was exactly that surreal. He came over, placed his hand on the back of my chair, and leaned in to introduce himself. Numbers were exchanged and after many texts later, a date was set. He was to meet me at my house, to pick me up I assumed, and we planned to drive one town over to have dinner and catch a movie. You know, totally normal first date type activity.

I happened to be outside in the front yard when he pulled in the driveway and was immediately taken aback by the car he was driving. Look, I try really hard not to be a judgmental person, I promise. But this thing looked like it had come straight off the crack house block. It was bonded together by mismatched paint and parts that had clearly been taken from another vehicle. The muffler didn't work, so I could hear the car coming when he was within a half mile of my house. Worst of all, there was a doughnut on the front passenger side tire.

I made a serious conscious effort not to let my shock show on my face and instead looked right past the car and met his eyes as he stepped into the driveway coming toward me. Ladies, let's be honest and real here for a moment—what I did in the coming minutes and hours was ignore every red flag in the book by overcompensating and immediately starting to craft excuses for this date of mine.

We all do. We want to give the benefit of the doubt. We don't want our excitement to be crushed and we don't want to be let down. We want to believe that somewhere in these men, that are not our men, there is a silver lining that if we just participate in the act long enough it will reveal itself.

There I was, making excuses before we even embraced in a hug. He is probably fixing this car up and it was blocking his ability to get his *real* car out of the drive, yeah that must be it. What other reason would make sense? Clearly he can't drive us thirty miles one way to our final destination with a donut on his car.

After we hugged and said our hellos, he said to me, "Sorry, but I won't be able to drive tonight. I was hoping to get the tire replaced today, but things just didn't work out."

"Oh, no problem," I said with my most fake overcompensating voice. "We will drive my car. Seriously, I do not mind."

I told him I needed to grab my keys and my purse from inside and turned toward the house. He said to me, "Nice house, how much does it rent for?" I turned back toward him and said, "Thanks. I own the home." I can still, to this day, over a decade later, see the look that washed across his face. He replied with an empty, "Oh," and that was that.

Something about this reaction, not the words, but his look, annoyed me. It ate at me and how I wish I would have the balls to call him out on it, but oh no—I was still in denial land, although another red flag had just smacked me square between the eyes. In the three short minutes since he pulled in my driveway, I had accumulated a stack of red flags. I chose to fold them neatly away, blissfully ignoring them and went on with the date.

Within the first ten minutes of the drive, we were talking about cell phones and service providers. He told me he was thinking about changing providers and asked who I used. I told him and mentioned I had never had any issues with service and recommended them. Then he asked, "How much do you pay a month?" I said, "Oh, I am not sure, I don't…" that was all I could get out of my mouth before he let out a half-hearted grunt and said, "Oh, your ex pays for your cell phone, too?"

I was floored. Let's just say I am a very prideful person. I have worked hard my entire life and take offense (right, wrong, or indifferent) at someone suggesting I do not pay my own way. I cleared my throat and with a smile, I said, "Actually, no, the company I work for pays for my cell bill." I kept my eyes fixed straight ahead as the final of the red flags jammed itself down my throat. I had to choke this one down. I knew something was off, and was really unsure what to do. I decided I was already in it so I may as well carry on and held in tight reserve a smidge of hope that he would catch on to the uncomfortable annoyance of my body language and turn this thing around. He did not.

During dinner I morphed from a date to a therapist. No, not really. I didn't change, but he perceived me as such as the baggage began to spew relentlessly from his mouth. He told me about this ex-wife, how long they had been married, how many kids they had, the square footage of the house they had built together that she now was the primary resident of, how her family was all well-to-do and had bailed her out and left him hanging out to dry. Nothing that had occurred was his fault and he had lost everything because of her, including his home.

Ding Ding Ding! Here was the animosity about me owning my home.

I was very familiar with talking about exes. I did it with my girlfriends often, but this just felt wrong in so many ways. But again, I listened intently and inserted advice and affirmations when appropriate. I am not naïve, and I know that men, just as frequently as women, can get stuck with the blunt end of the stick in divorce. I continued to force myself to listen with empathy and understanding.

It was when we were almost done with dinner that we began talking about our jobs and what we did for a living. The circumstances around his job sounded strangely like those that surrounded his marriage. His supervisor had demoted him from his former position for a situation that occurred that he was not directly responsible for, and he wasn't able to work as many hours and make as much money, and blah blah blah. I honestly have no idea what else he said about the situation. By this point I was done even maintaining eye contact.

We did, for whatever reason, continue to the movies, but I couldn't concentrate on the big screen. I just wanted to be at home and have never been happier to get there once we were back. He tried to kiss me when he walked me to the door, and I think he planned to come in.

I was swift, stuck my key in the lock with a quick twist, I was on the other side of the door frame pushing the door closed, wishing him goodnight before he knew what had happened. Needless to say, I never spoke to him again.

There were a few valuable lessons, however, that I took from that night. When we, the society of divorced people, reenter the society of dating we are changed humans. Dating is no longer what it was when we were Pre-Marriage, when we were looking for a good time. The people you interact with have been through their own personal version of hell. Some walk through it gracefully and exit unscathed on the other side, and then there are those who stumble and crawl, bitter and cold, never seeming to rediscover themselves.

There were times during these years that I am sure I didn't come across as my best self, because I was trying to find and reinvent myself. There were months and years during that process that were messier than others, and I have no doubt I exuded that disarray to others.

I was too scared to take a look deep down at what I wanted because I was afraid I would never find it. I wanted to find a partner, someone who would walk beside me—not in front of me and not behind me—beside me. I really had no clue what that looked like at the time and to be honest, I do not even think such a thing existed.

I would soon find out that I was wrong.

Frayed Yarn

The first time I saw him he was sitting in a conference room awaiting an interview with the company where I worked. In hindsight, it is so strange that I have a very vivid memory of seeing him for the first time, even to this very day, more than a decade later. His back was turned but I could tell he was dressed to the nines, full suit and tie, shiny shoes, and a posh short haircut.

A few weeks later when he moved into the office next to mine, I decided to walk over and introduce myself. He was unpacking boxes and preoccupied so I lightly tapped on the door to get his attention. This was the first time I saw his face. He was serious. I couldn't put my finger at that moment on what exactly was this seriousness was, but it was real.

I extended my hand, noting that I just wanted to say hello to my new neighbor and introduce myself. His face softened and I noticed a pair of the bluest eyes I had ever seen. Behind that serious exterior, I saw a glimpse of a human, a real live human.

As time passed, I learned a few notable details about this human. He had been a Drill Instructor in the Marine Corp; no wonder he had a serious demeanor. He had moved his family here from Texas; he was married with two kids. After being in a few meetings with him I formed the opinion he was simply a quiet person and he was definitely reserved, keeping to himself. Something about him just felt heavy to me. I observed but asked no questions.

Right away he was sent on an assignment to a field office that was 200 miles away for his first few months on the job. So aside from our initial meeting, we had very little interaction. The time he was in the office right beside me, I hardly even remembered he was there, keeping to himself on the other side of his closed office door.

It wasn't until several months later, when the assignment ended and he was back to being my neighbor full time, that I noticed a distinct change in his demeanor. He seemed almost lighter somehow, maybe a little distracted in a sad and sometimes searching way. The lightness in his presence felt different. However at that time didn't even realize I was actively aware. It is only in hindsight that I realize I was noticing these things.

In retrospect, I can remember the first time I actively paid attention. It was during a business meeting where I first saw him step into a leadership role and address the room. This day was no different than every other Monday that had come before. We would kick off the week with a Team Meeting. But this was notably the first time that I really saw him—even though I had seen him, met him, exchanged pleasantries with him. On that day, in that conference room, I saw who he was, and if I am being honest, I liked what I saw.

I would soon learn he and his wife had separated and she had left him and the boys to go back to Texas. As it turns out, the marriage had been rocky for quite some time and the move from Texas to Tennessee was just enough to tip the scales completely out of balance for the two of them, exposing the issues that lay far beyond the surface of the relationship.

I didn't learn all of this right away. It was months later that we found ourselves at the bar across the street from our office. It was the typical hang out, that bar across the street, once or twice a month a large part of the office staff would congregate after work, partake in some adult beverages, and blow off some steam.

This particular night, the last of the coworkers who had joined us after work were heading home, but neither he nor I seemed to have the same sense of urgency to leave. My kids were with their dad, so I was not eager to get home to the empty house that was waiting, and I could sense a similar hesitation in him. We agreed to have one more and stayed a bit longer.

That was when the conversation started, a dialogue between two people, that felt like it had been waiting an eternity to be had.

It was clear to me as he started to talk that he needed to open up, as if in confession. He had not confided his situation to anyone, other than probing family members who had called to find out why she had shown back up in Texas…alone. It was an unspoken mutual understanding we had almost instantly. He felt like he could confide in me and I felt it oddly therapeutic to let him do so.

It is important to note here that this was not the normal for either of us, him to confide in me, who was truly little more than a stranger, and me to be so drawn to someone else's pain. For months we were intertwined in our stories, our losses, our wins, our dreams, and our goals for the future.

We found a certain trust in the space between us where we could meet each other with the vulnerability of our words and not be met with judgement. Our roles were clear—I served as a relationship mentor offering him a female perspective to try to mend his marriage and in return, he offered me male perspective on how to feel my fears around pursuing my educations and elevating myself in my own career. This encouragement, support, and trust was what solidified our friendship, one we both knew would ultimately last for all our lives. We both agree to this very day, almost a decade later, that even if we hadn't ended up together, we would have remained friends, always.

After several months had passed and his separation continued to drag on and appeared to be at an impasse, I could feel myself looking forward to the time we spent together. We literally would talk for hours. I had never met anyone who I could engage with on that sort of level. I was starting to become more attached to him and the place he held in my life, which concerned me. I knew intellectually this could and would never work out like that.

I mean, this man had confided in me how much he loved his wife and he would until the meat fell off her bones. He wanted nothing more in this world than for their marriage to be mended and things to be as they once had been. Again, I knew this in my brain, but I could feel my heart was starting to get in the way and this was a problem on so many levels.

I took action, quite possibly the first real selfless action I had ever taken in my entire life, and encouraged him to reach out to his wife. I told him he should avoid putting the focus on the why and the how of where they were today and try to appeal to the feelings they had that landed them together in the first place. To let her know how badly he missed her and tell her he just wanted her to be there with him, to come home.

He made the phone call that very night and his plea, my words, hit her straight in the heart. Before I knew it there were plans in the works for her to move back to Tennessee and to give the marriage another shot.

I am not sure what was harder, the time leading up to her coming back or the six weeks that she was here. I was happy she was coming back and a bit relieved at the notion that this put things in a very simplified perspective.

On an intellectual level I knew and understood the feelings that were creeping into my heart and taking over my mind had to be put down. But in my heart, I was scattered and confused. I had no idea what this meant for our friendship or how I would fit into the equation, if I was like an awkward third wheel, trying to attach itself to a bicycle.

The way I felt and the concerns I had were the least of the articles for consideration here, and I knew it. I took those feeling and thoughts and I dropped them. Every single notion, every perception, every sentiment, every question, dropped like a hot potato…at least outwardly. Inwardly, it took some time. However, I knew the reality, and I worked to put those feelings and complications to the side.

My heart was still on the mend when he told me he missed me, our conversations, and my company, and in the same breath he told me she was leaving to go back to Texas. They had tried their best and given their love and lives together one last try, but it no longer fit for either of them. They had come to a mutual agreement that the marriage was over, and they would move forward with a divorce.

I could see the pleading in his eyes as he spoke and knew that neither of us really understood what this meant. As the pieces of life as he knew it crumbled, I stayed at a safe distance, only stepping in occasionally to pick a select few up. It no doubt would have been easier to walk away, to distance myself from the pain he was experiencing. I did not walk away, but rather I walked with him, beside him, right through the middle of the sorrow, loss, and ultimate death of that marriage. And while it was hard and I questioned so many things so many times during that journey, I have never been so sure of any decision in my life.

You see my fairy tale did not come wrapped in silk and lace with a dreamy Prince Charming standing on the other side. My fairy tale was wrapped in hardships, broken hearts, unselfish compassion, and mostly friendship. This doesn't make for a good bedtime story and it may have made you a little uncomfortable to read it. I get it. But this is my truth, this is how it unfolded for me, and if I would have had my head in the clouds looking for the white knight, I would have missed it.

I have learned that for those of us who have failed attempts at sharing our lives with another, love is messy, frayed, and tangled like a ball of yarn that has been unraveled and rewrapped over decades of time. Our hearts have been broken, our hope has been crushed, and our dreams have become colorless. We have long since lost naivety around love, partnership, and promises of forever. We understand the implications of being in relationship with another and the work that is required, both internally and externally. We come prepared to step into the ring and labor for the person who shines color back into our dreams.

And sometimes we step in without even realizing how we got there.

We went to Jared's

My dad gave me a riding lawn mower the first summer after my divorce. It was an old Craftsman, a bit rusty and worn, a piece of duct tape on the seat to mend the wear of time. He had gotten it from a friend who had bought a new mower and had no more use for this old gem. You've heard it said—one man's trash, another man's treasure. That old mower might have appeared on the surface that it was ready to retire, but when I heard her fire up for the first time, I knew she wasn't done just yet. Let me be clear—she was a finicky beast who demanded a combination of precise settings and a bit of encouragement to start up.

The first Saturday morning I tried to start her on my own, nothing happened when I turned the key. My heart sank as I entertained the realization I would be pulling the push mower from the shed. It would take double the time to get the job done, not to mention the energy it would inevitably suck from me. Time and energy, not two things a single mom has an overabundance of on her hands, as we've already discussed.

I kept adjusting the choke and slowly cranked the acceleration from the tortoise setting methodically moving toward rabbit as I turned the key. After a series of tries I found the right spot and she fired up, just like she did on the day I got her. My heart was full, I was thankful to have a riding mower and more grateful that I was able to figure it out on my own. Every single time I would get on that lawn mower I would start with a sense of dread, afraid that would be the time she wouldn't start. But ultimately, every time I was able to get her to fire and my sense of pride intensified. I was learning to depend on myself.

I had become attached to my identity as this thriving woman who could do everything on her own. I walked through the depths of worry and fear and had learned how I could trust myself how to make things work, all the things. Tighten the pipe under the sink so it wouldn't leak, unstop the toilet when it was jammed, replace a hot water heater, assemble and move furniture, repair door knobs and locks, caulking around showers and tubs, landscaping, you name it, and at some point I had figured out how to, A) do it myself, or B) pay to have it done.

I would not have a real understanding of just how large my attachment to depending on myself had become until I found someone I cared for deeply. I would love to tell you that the transition from being on my own all those years to being in a relationship with a person I cared for intensely was seamless, smooth as silk. However, nothing could be further from the truth.

The ugly truth is I did not know how to see myself as whole stepping into a relationship with someone who only needed me for me. All he wanted from me was my companionship, my partnership, and my friendship. And I was unsure of who I was without feeling the need to prove myself to him. I had an overwhelming sense of needing him to understand I was perfectly capable of doing it all on my own. Intellectually, I knew he didn't care, he wanted to do it with me. Do life with me. But this independent self-reliant version of whom I had become did not need that. Or did she?

But our relationship would not and could not meet its full potential if I would have held onto that version of myself. The closer we became and the deeper our relationship rooted, the more I could feel myself in an internal tug of war. I wanted to step into this new phase of my life. I wanted to believe I could have this relationship. I wanted to trust in him and trust in us. But my "want" was no match for my fear. It wasn't until we had started to talk about marriage that I hit an impasse, a true crossroads that exposed my fear like none other.

We had skirted the topic many times. We agreed that eventually we would get married. It was easy to talk about, however, as we all know, talking and doing are two highly dissimilar animals. And neither of us seemed in a hurry to rush down the aisle. Most of the times I brought it up it was to pick at him because I thought he was just as uncertain as I was, in a state of complete hesitation. But then one day he called my bluff.

It was the Christmas Season, and per the usual, the commercials for jewelry were numerous. There was one that really stood out, with the infamous tagline, "He went to Jared's." We were doing some

Christmas shopping when we passed by the store and I sounded off in my most gimmicky commercial voice, "*He* went to Jared's." He looked at me dead in the eye and said, "*He* wants you to have the ring you want, so why don't *we* go to Jared's." In than instant, I knew he was no longer holding back and it became abundantly clear that I now stood alone in hesitation.

Walking through the doors of the store I was immediately on sensory overload. The room felt too bright, too sparkly, too crowded, too loud, too hot, and too small. We were barely inside the doors before we were greeted by the man who would be directing us on our journey through Jared's treasures. I could barely hear the man's words over the buzzing in my head and was keenly aware of how hot my feet had become. The soles of my feet and the palms of my hands were both wet with nervous perspiration.

Somehow, we made it to a set of chairs that faced a display of engagement rings and the questions began.

Did I prefer gold or silver?
Did I have a specific cut in mind?
How many carets were we looking for?
When would we be getting married?

Although the exact details are murky in my memory, I am pretty sure it was the last of the questions that pushed me over the edge. What I can remember clearly is I looked the man straight in the eyes and said to him, "We are not going to be buying anything today and I do not want to waste your time. Please go help someone that is ready." And with that I stood and made a beeline for the front door.

When I made it outside, I took a deep breath of the cool air and felt the tension release from my body, unsure exactly what I had just experienced. I felt vulnerable, nervous, and exposed. The presence of fear started at the tip of my head and vibrated down my body to the soles of my feet. That fear that lived deep inside had risen to the surface like a dragon peeking his head out of the depths of his dark and dank cave. You can't *unsee* the dragon when you've unleashed him for the entire world to witness. More importantly than anything, the man who loved me had witnessed it as well, and to be honest, was more confused than I was.

I was left with a decision to make, a simple decision, really. Would I choose to hold on to the version of myself, the girl who had to prove to everyone that she needed no one, or would I accept that I wanted to be the girl who could depend on someone.

We have spent the majority of this book exploring how we can stand on our own two feet and show up for ourselves when we have no one to stand with us. And while I stand firm in the notion that there are few more valuable lessons for a single mom to learn than how to stand on her own two feet, it is equally important to be able to recognize when you have someone in your life who wants to stand beside you.

Fear and love stand on opposite sides of a common axis. Both there because they have earned their right to be present on scales of emotions that drive our lives. However, there is one important difference to note when it comes to differentiating the two, and that is potential. Fear, while strong and mighty in her own right, has no real potential to offer. Her existence is filled with unanswered questions, anxiety, worry, doubt, and unease. She has nothing more to offer us in the long term than gray hair and settling for less than we deserve. Love, however, offers a bounty of potential. Her existence is bliss, affection, becoming, evolving, caring, and divine. Love is greater than fear.

So, my dear reader, whenever you are in a position to make a choice, choose love. Every. Single. Time.

Tool #10: Keep Your Tools Sharp

Honing

From the very first outlines of this book, I knew I wanted to give the reader ten tools, ten chapters. It was a nice, round number, and certainly I could identify the top ten that were of most importance to implement. No matter what, I was always coming up one short. I kept writing of course, knowing that one day it would click and I would finally identify that missing link, and it did.

We were in the kitchen prepping some meat and veggies for grilling. I was digging around in the fridge trying to find the squash when I heard the sound behind me. Metal on metal, grind after grind, pass after pass, slow and steady sharpening of a blade. My hubby had pulled out the knife sharpener and was slowly running the blade of our paring knife along the edge to sharpen it.

I froze and turned to him, like a deer in headlights, and asked slowly, "What are you doing?"

Obviously confused by my question and more concerned by my demeanor, he stated slowly back, "I am sharpening the knife, so we get a nice clean cut."

And there it was. The idea struck me as abruptly as a lightning rod striking a metal pole.

Honing—to sharpen, to refine, to perfect over a period of time.

A blunt tool, much like a dull knife, can be dangerous because it requires more pressure to be exerted when cutting, which increases the risk of injury. It takes a lot less energy and effort to cut through a veggie or piece of meat with a sharpened blade. It is much the same with your metaphorical tools. They are much more effective when kept sharpened and ready for action.

Each tool we have covered within the chapters of this book have offered a fresh approach to the principles in our lives that we may have forgotten to notice or simply not found the time for in a very long time. It is easy to allow ourselves to fall into patterns and to let life happen to us, especially when the roads we are traveling are bumpy and uncomfortable. We have to dig deep and find our intention, even if it is just a little each day, to be mindful and deliberate. It is not an overnight change, it will take persistence, it will require your patience, and it will take your dedication to refining the approach to each tool over a period of time until you find exactly what works for you.

Through the principles and tools we've covered, we have embraced acceptance and understanding that there are no quick fixes or alternatives for the difficult situations we will encounter. We have learned how to stand in the pain, knowing there are lessons to be learned if we can quiet ourselves and pay close attention. Life lessons are found within the hardships, the loss, and our discomfort of every day occurrences. In every single moment there is a valuable jewel there if we can switch our mindset to see it. If we do not make ourselves aware and intentional to identify the value in the painful situations, then we will lose those invaluable lessons forever.

Also important to reiterate, there are no purchases necessary for any of the things we have covered and it is set up that way for a very simple reason. You already have what you need to shift your path; the majority of the work comes down to a decision to make a mindset shift. Do not overanalyze the actions that are necessary. Just give yourself the grace to step into them, simply trying on a different thought process for a moment, keep what works for you and discard what doesn't.

There are a few honing techniques I want to leave you with that are important to keep close, intact, with the tools we have covered to ensure you stay on the most productive path.

Obsessions and Illusions

As you feel your way through this book, it will challenge your perceptions of both your past life and future living. However, it is infinitely crucial to note there is a fine balance you need to maintain with your focus on the present, the here, the now. The past is behind you and can be used as a great history lesson for what you have learned through previous experiences. The future is an exciting prospect, especially when reading a self-development book filled with options just waiting for you to try to implement on your own journey. It is often easy to forget to hit pause and take a moment to appreciate where you stand in the present.

Take a breath, raise your gaze, open your eyes wide, and take it all in. The air that fills your lungs, the breeze that touches your cheeks, the sounds of birds chirping in the trees, the clouds that paint the perfect backdrop seamlessly in the sky, the grass growing from the ground, and the heart beating inside your chest.

Our time here is limited, and though we know this, we still spend so much of our time obsessing about things that happened in our past or lost in an illusion of what the future might hold. These obsessions and illusions are robbing you of being present with yourself, with your family, with your friends, with your kids, and with your life. Even if where you are today is filled with heartache and unknowns, look around you. Stop and give yourself a moment to consider and ponder that the moment you are in is here to teach you something.

Finding meaning in this moment, this experience, this challenge is key to helping you to ground yourself in the present. It is counterproductive to waste your precious time trying to rail against what is behind you or to fixate on what is to come. Through the simple tools in this book you have learned how to plan and maximize the most simplistic of ways to rise from whatever hard circumstance you find yourself in. Embrace where you are now as there is no place for you left in the past or in the future. Don't miss the here and now because you are stuck there.

To find meaning in the moment, you can ask yourself a series of very simple questions:

What is my why?
What is important to me?
How do I want my kids to remember this moment?
What am I willing to struggle for?
What am I grateful for?

These five questions are really good reminders for all of us to ask ourselves every single day. They help remind us what is truly important and why. Everything else is just noise in the background, and with a bit of intention and practice you will be able to bring focus to what is actually important—the here and the now.

Flexibility, Ebbing, and Flowing

When I was fifteen years old when my grandmother gave me some of the most simplistic truth I have ever been handed in this life. I had just experienced my first real heartbreak and literally thought life was over. I was "teenage devastated," going through a breakup with a boyfriend. We have all had those times at some point in our adolescence where we fall hard and fast and think the relationship we landed in is the answer to all our hopes and dreams, right?

This was one of those times for me. I was head over heels for this boy, so much so that I wouldn't go outside for fear of missing his call when I was at my grandmother's house. Circa mid-90's, the only phones my grandmother had in her house were the ones attached to the back porch wall, right off the kitchen, and the rotary that set beside her bedside. I know she noticed my obsession with waiting for his call on Saturday nights, but she didn't comment. She stood by and watched, being sure to be close enough to catch me when it all came crashing down around my feet.

And it did—it crashed hard. He told me before second period that he wanted to break up with me. I was stunned and didn't understand why. When I saw him walking with another girl before sixth period, it all came together to form a perfect picture of understanding in my teenage mind. I waited until I made it to my grandmother's house after school before I let myself fall completely apart.

I will never forget sitting on the floor of the bathroom, crying, my back against the tub that I had bathed in so many times as a kid, sobbing uncontrollably. My grandmother took a seat on the edge of the bathtub and gently rubbed my back as I repeated over and over, "I just don't understand." I guess that down deep in my heart of hearts I wanted her to explain, to impart some wisdom that would take the pain away just as abruptly as it had come. But she couldn't take the hurt from me. Instead, she sat with me and offered this bit of advice:

"Life has a tendency to ebb and flow, and most times it is easier to just let go and see where the flow takes you."

In complete fairness, I didn't grasp the power of this statement or the practicality of the principle at that particular time. Even today I have to pause and remind myself of the unpredictability of life and natural progression of events in our lives. It is only to be accepted that things are not always going to go the way we have planned, and situations will not work out the way we might have hoped they would.

It is important to be mindful, aware, intentional to keep an open mind. The changes you are going through and the reality of a situation may look completely different from what you had envisioned, but that doesn't mean it is a recipe for catastrophe. When the unplanned and unforeseen occur, they are accompanied by an opportunity. Always.

So I will ask you:

Are you looking for opportunity?

Are you willing to shift your expectations?

Are you accepting of the new people, places, and things that are introduced by this redirection?

Are you holding on to how you wish things were rather than accepting how things are?

Be brave and bold and hold yourself accountable. Resist the temptation to tighten your body physically. Remember your breath—your number one super power. Breathe in deep and do not act; allow yourself the chance to truly evaluate the situation without measuring it beside some preconceived notion you had of how it "might have been" or was "supposed to be." It is truly okay to feel disappointment when things do not go as we think they will. What is not okay is to allow yourself to become paralyzed by it.

There is one thing that is certain in this wild ride called life. Shit is not going to go your way, people are going to hurt your feelings, and you are for certain going to get your heart broken. Unless you are a complete hermit living in a cave alone, there is no way to avoid this.

You can't change the circumstances, but you can influence and control your reaction to them. Flexibility is not only important for your peace of mind, reducing stress, and mitigating negative impact to your mental health, it is also the key to your success and creating that progressive momentum we have covered in this book. Chin up, sister. Look to the bright side of the situation and you will see it is always waiting there for you to discover.

Humility and Pride

Being a Single Mom is one of the most humbling things you will likely ever do in your life. However, there is a difference between being humble and practicing humility.

For the vast majority of the Single Mom population, we did not plan for things to end up this way, to be raising our kids alone or co-parenting. We did not plan for our marriages to fail, our significant other to pass away, or the father of our kids to simply decide to opt out of the parenting role.

These situations have presented themselves, in many cases, with a shockwave that has brought us to our knees, knocking the breath from our lungs and suddenly painting our world in dark shades of blues and blacks. We are disoriented, alone, and afraid, but we know we can't quit.

Giving up is never an option for the strongminded Single Mom.

Some days are easier than others, but nonetheless she moves forward and with every new day, finds it easier to persist. Her situations have given her a new perspective on life and an understanding of just how fragile relationships are and how temporary situations can be. She certainly had to endure some struggles to find herself on the rocky ground where she rests her feet today. And every day that follows, she will find herself holding fast, standing guard over her territory, ruling with cool, steadfast confidence. Her situation has introduced her to a new level of modesty, her persistence has kept her grounded, and her determination has imprinted the sheer definition of being humble onto her heart.

But we must remember to actively practice humility to keep growing, striving, and moving ourselves and family forward. To do this, we have to check ourselves as it pertains to our pride. Pride is the enemy to humility, the one thing that can stand in our way and prevent us from experiencing growth and progression in our lives.

We are not talking about a high sense of self-worth or a feeling of excitement that arises with our accomplishments. It is very healthy to receive praise and to allow yourself to feel the satisfaction that comes with positive results from hard work and dedication. Pride is a fuel of sorts for our emotions. This emotion is important because it encourages us to persist in our endeavors, which reinforces the momentum to keep propelling forward. From this perspective, pride is actually a virtue. But like most principles in life, pride has two sides to the proverbial coin.

What I am speaking about specifically in this section is the pride we hold onto when our ego has been bruised and we feel like we might not be in control of our circumstances. This type of pride can create an aversion to vulnerability and make us feel that we need to create a guard to keep ourselves safe. We have to be careful not to build up a barrier around ourselves in an attempt to maintain an illusion of competence and control.

For example, this type of pride might make us hesitate to ask for help when we really need it. The thought of reaching out brings up an onslaught of shame and insecurity. We hesitate because we correlate our own ability with the need for assistance and question if we are "less than" if we feel the need to lean on others. Or worse yet, someone proactively offers their help to us and we pause because we think we should be able to do it all on our own.

I have to tell you this is an area where I still continue to struggle to this very day. I have no doubt missed out on opportunities to enrich my relationships, incrementally improve life experiences, and create more possibilities in my own life because of my inability to ask for or receive help from others. My ego tends to become so wrapped in this self-created identity of being this strong woman who doesn't need anyone or anything to thrive. I often forget who I am without this sense of pride. I have to remind myself that even without my accomplishments, I am still a person worthy of love and accolades. Everything I have accomplished on my own could have been magnified by an undefinable extent if I had allowed myself to be less prideful and ask those around me for help.

So remember this as you move forward with your tools: be humble, practice humility, and swallow your pride, even if you choke a bit on it at first.

Printed in Great Britain
by Amazon